ANCHOR BABIES AND
THE CHALLENGE OF
BIRTHRIGHT CITIZENSHIP

ANCHOR BABIES AND
THE CHALLENGE OF
BIRTHRIGHT CITIZENSHIP

LEO R. CHAVEZ

stanford briefs
An Imprint of Stanford University Press
Stanford, California

Stanford University Press
Stanford, California

Printed in the United States of America
on acid-free, archival-quality paper

Library of Congress Cataloging-in-Publication Data

Names: Chavez, Leo R. (Leo Ralph), author.
Title: Anchor babies and the challenge of birthright citizenship / Leo R.
  Chavez.
Description: Stanford, California : Stanford Briefs, an imprint of
  Stanford University Press, 2017. | Includes bibliographical references.
Identifiers: LCCN 2017033752 | ISBN 9781503605091 (pbk. : alk. paper) |
  ISBN 9781503605268 (ebook)
Subjects: LCSH: Citizenship—United States. | Children of illegal
  aliens—Legal status, laws, etc.—United States. | Children of
  immigrants—Legal status, laws, etc.—United States. | United States.
  Constitution. 14th Amendment. | United States—Emigration and
  immigration—Government policy.
Classification: LCC JK1759 C6 2017 | DDC 323.6/2—dc23

LC record available at https://lccn.loc.gov/2017033752

Typeset by Classic Typography in 10/13 Adobe Garamond

CONTENTS

For Peter and Makiko Ota,
who live with honor and dignity

Donald Trump launched his campaign to become the 45th president of the United States by disparaging Mexican immigrants: "When Mexico sends its people, they're not sending their best. They're not sending you. They're not sending you. They're sending people that have lots of problems, and they're bringing those problems with us. They're bringing drugs. They're bringing crime. They're rapists. And some, I assume, are good people."[1]

As shocking and incendiary as these characterizations of Mexican immigrants were, Trump's less noticed comments about U.S.-born children of undocumented immigrants also deserved notice. Mr. Trump called these children "anchor babies," a term that had become part of public discourse only a decade earlier, to suggest these children were not "real" citizens because their parents were undocumented immigrants who bore these children in the United States in order to get citizenship for themselves. In other words, anchor babies are part of an alleged conspiracy to take advantage of the United States. Trump said anchor babies might not be citizens or have a legal right to live in the United States. "I'd much rather find out whether or not 'anchor babies' are citizens because a lot of people don't think they are."[2]

1

So-called anchor babies are born in the United States and thus acquire citizenship as a birthright. Birthright citizenship is one of the pillars of our nation's laws and one of the key values that make America great. To be born in the United States makes one a citizen and symbolizes an inclusiveness often lacking in many countries of the world. Was Trump really questioning the citizenship of people born in the United States?

Birthright citizenship is based on the principle of *jus soli*, which means "right to soil." Jus soli is the right to claim citizenship as a result of being born in the territory of a state. Although a key principle in American legal history, jus soli or birthright citizenship has not always been bestowed on all those born on American soil. Native Americans, African American slaves, and the children of nonwhite immigrants were left out for much of our history. The Fourteenth Amendment to the U.S. Constitution guarantees citizenship to all babies born in the United States: "All persons born or naturalized in the United States, and subject to the jurisdiction thereof, are citizens of the United States and of the State wherein they reside." Even after acquiring birthright citizenship, the children of immigrants and other stigmatized ethnic or racial groups often found their citizenship diminished by laws and social attitudes about their deservingness and belonging to the nation.

The children of immigrants have long held a tenuous position in American society.[3] This deep and contentious history is sometimes hard to square in a country that prides itself on being "a nation of immigrants." For over two hundred years Americans have argued over the place of the children of immigrants. At times, these debates have produced vitriolic political rhetoric and nativism, resulting in some racial groups being characterized as perpetual foreigners and "alien citizens."[4] Restrictive immigration policies and unconstitutional actions targeting citizen children of immigrants have led to the repatriation of Mexican Americans to

Mexico during the Great Depression and the internment of Japanese Americans during World War II.[5]

"Anchor baby" is a decidedly more provocative and offensive term than "birthright citizenship."[6] Calling the children of undocumented parents anchor babies underscores that *these* people do not deserve to be citizens; they are "accidental citizens" and "citizens who do not belong."[7] It perpetuates the idea of a conspiracy by undocumented immigrants who choose to have a U.S.-citizen baby to be able to apply, someday, for his or her family's legal residence.

The term "anchor baby" first appeared in the 1980s, although in an academic rather than a political context. A 1987 article in the *Los Angeles Times Magazine* profiled Kenji Ima and Jeanne Nidorf, two San Diego State University professors, and their research on troubled Southeast Asian teens. "They [Southeast Asian teens] are 'anchor children,' saddled with the extra burden of having to attain a financial foothold in America to sponsor family members who remain in Vietnam."[8]

I also used the anchor metaphor in *Shadowed Lives: Undocumented Immigrants in American Society*.[9] My book, based primarily on research I conducted in the 1980s and early 1990s, examined the many social and cultural linkages to U.S. society found among undocumented families and their children, which over time increased their desire to stay in the United States no matter their citizenship status. "Most of the parents I interviewed said their children did not want to return to Mexico or Central America. This perception of their children's attitudes helps anchor parents in the United States." This anchoring effect helped me understand why undocumented immigrants might stay longer in the United States than they had originally intended.[10]

But this effect had a completely different meaning from what ultimately emerged with the term "anchor baby" in the early 2000s. Take, for example, conservative pundit Michelle Malkin's comments about anchor babies in her blog entry for June 13, 2004:

During my book tour across the country for *Invasion*, this issue [of anchor babies] came up time and again. In the Southwest, everyone has a story of heavily pregnant women crossing the Mexican border to deliver their "anchor babies." At East Coast hospitals, tales of South Korean "obstetric tourists" abound. (An estimated 5,000 South Korean anchor babies are born in the US every year.) And, of course, there's a terrorism angle.[11]

In 2005, Malkin again linked birthright citizenship to undocumented immigration and post–9/11 fears of terrorism: "Clearly, the custom of granting automatic citizenship at birth to children of tourists, and temporary workers . . . and to countless 'anchor babies' delivered by illegal aliens on American soil, undermines the integrity of citizenship—not to mention national security. . . . The citizenship clause has evolved into a magnet for alien law breakers and a shield for terrorist infiltrators and enemy combatants."[12] By linking U.S.-citizen babies to "illegal aliens," Malkin attempts to undercut the legitimacy of those babies.[13]

As the rhetoric around anchor babies heated up, citizens suddenly found themselves targets of anti-immigrant discourse and even policies. In 2010, Florida's higher education administrators began treating so-called anchor babies as nonresidents of the state if they could not prove their parents were legal immigrants.[14] These citizens would have to pay the much more expensive nonresident college tuition ($27,936 a year at the time), compared to what other "resident citizens" ($5,700) paid, even if they had spent their entire lives in Florida and had gone to primary and secondary schools in the state. At the time, the anchor baby rhetoric was heating up and there was a bill in Congress to repeal the Fourteenth Amendment and birthright citizenship. However, rather than wait for congressional action, the Florida Board of Education used its own policy to effectively repeal the protections of the Fourteenth Amendment. Critics filed a class action lawsuit claiming the policy violated the equal protection clause of the Fourteenth Amendment. On August 31, 2012, U.S. district judge Michael Moore, finding the practice unconstitutional, ordered Florida public colleges to stop charging U.S.-born children of undocumented immigrants out-of-state tuition.[15] From nine to twelve thousand U.S.-citizen students were immediately affected by the ruling, and yet they had to endure what must have seemed a form of punishment for their parents' decision to come to the United States.

Six years later, even candidates for president of the United States routinely referred to anchor babies in a pejorative sense. Donald Trump told his supporters that women were crossing the border to deliver their anchor babies and that Americans were "disgusted when a woman who's nine months pregnant walks across the border, has a baby, and you have to take care of that baby for the next 85 years."[16]

The relatively sudden appearance of the term "anchor baby" had dictionaries scrambling, and stumbling, to define it. In 2011, the *American Heritage Dictionary* defined "anchor baby" as "a child born to a noncitizen mother in a country that grants automatic citizenship to children born on its soil, especially such a child born to parents seeking to secure eventual citizenship for themselves and often other members of their family."[17] However, the dictionary's definition was criticized almost immediately for writing as if the anchor baby actually existed objectively and not as a pejorative, politically constructed concept. Responding to the criticism, the *American Heritage Dictionary* revised its definition on its website: "Anchor baby, *n. Offensive.* Used as a disparaging term for a child born to a noncitizen mother in a country that grants automatic citizenship to children born on its soil, especially when the child's birthplace is thought to have been chosen in order to improve the mother's or other relatives' chances of securing eventual citizenship."[18]

In the heated political discourse over anchor babies, both these definitions could hold true depending on who was using the term. But even these two opposing definitions do not capture the negative stereotypes that would become associated with the anchor baby image: an undeserving citizen, a burden on medical care and social services, a racial threat through the "browning of America," a harbinger of environmental disaster, and ultimately a foreigner.[19] In other words, to those using the term as a political dog whistle, anchor babies symbolize a threat to the American way of life.

Three questions frame the three chapters of this book: First, how has the term "anchor baby" been put to use over time in public discourse and debates about birthright citizenship? As "anchor baby" appears with increasing frequency in the media, stories in the *Los Angeles Times* and *New York Times* can be used to highlight the contemporary politics over birthright citizenship. A key issue used to bolster the anchor baby characterization is that although the parents, and thus the babies, were in the United States, they were not "under the jurisdiction thereof," as required by the Fourteenth Amendment, because of their undocumented status. The anchor baby rhetoric, with its negative characterizations of the children of undocumented immigrants, constructs both deserving citizens and undeserving citizens.

Second, how have changes in the legal definition of citizenship affected the children of immigrants? Contemporary public discourse over anchor babies must be put into historical perspective. From colonial days to the Fourteenth Amendment to the U.S. Constitution, jus soli and what it means to be "under the jurisdiction" of the United States played key roles in determining citizenship. Even as birthright citizenship was seemingly settled by the Fourteenth Amendment and subsequent Supreme Court decisions, contestations over citizenship, especially pertaining to U.S. race relations and immigration, continued over the course of the 20th century and into the 21st century.

And third, in what ways do U.S.-born citizens still experience trauma in their everyday lives because they live in families with undocumented immigrants? Citizenship does not necessarily buffer these so-called anchor babies from forced family separation, economic hardships, unwanted exile, psychological depression, or a lack of academic achievement if a father, mother, or other family member is deported. U.S.-born children of undocumented immigrants find their citizenship diminished as a result of the anchor baby rhetoric and the social stigma it generates, as well as the tragedy they experience when family members are deported, or the hardship of living with the constant fear of deportation.

Whether considered anchor babies or full-fledged members of the nation through birthright citizenship, the children of immigrants are central to any exploration of citizenship in the United States. Citizenship alone is not enough to integrate the children of immigrants into the nation. Citizenship must be accompanied by a recognition that these children belong and deserve to be treated like all other members of society. Public discourse that questions their citizenship, raises issues such as whether they were born under the jurisdiction of the laws of the United States given their parents' immigration status, and threatens to eliminate their birthright citizenship undermines these children's personal sense of belonging as well as how they are viewed by the larger society. It marks them as internal "Others" who are not to be trusted, because they are "illegitimate," "suspect," and undeserving citizens. Down that path we should not go. History and contemporary societies are replete with examples of how creating discontented and excluded internal Others undermines social cohesion and can lead to social and legal violence. Examining the emergence and use of the anchor baby rhetoric exposes its basic weaknesses and ultimately its decidedly un-American sentiment.

1 UNDESERVING CITIZENS?

On June 22, 1974, Leonard F. Chapman Jr., commissioner of the Immigration and Naturalization Service, warned about immigrant fertility rates: "We're very close in this country to a zero population growth through births. As we get closer to that zero growth, immigration will become an even larger percentage of the population increase."[1] Then on July 4, 1977, *U.S. News & World Report*'s cover announced: "Time Bomb in Mexico: Why They'll Be No End to the Invasion by 'Illegals.'" The time bomb was the fertility rate of Mexican women. The relationship among immigration/invasion, demographic change, women, fertility, and children was clear and would frame public discourse on birthright citizenship and anchor babies up to the present.

Leonard Chapman and *U.S. News & World Report* were articulating a growing concern over increased immigration and demographic change. The Immigration and Nationality Act of 1965 removed national origin quotas that were instituted in the 1920s, which effectively reduced immigration from southern and eastern Europe and barred immigrants from most Asian countries. The 1965 immigration law put in place a family and labor preference system for immigration.[2] This essentially opened immigration to almost all countries in the world. The elimination of national origin quotas removed the legal preference for Europeans in our immigration policy, which in turn initiated changes in the nation's demographic profile.

Although the immigration law was not the only factor, 1965 marked the beginning of an increase in immigration. In 1960, Europeans accounted for 84 percent of immigrants to the United States. The ten largest immigrant groups in 1960 were primarily European: Italy (12.9%), Germany (10.2%), Canada (9.8%), United Kingdom (8.6%), Poland (7.7%), Soviet Union (7.1%), Mexico (5.9%), Ireland (3.5%), Austria (3.1%), and Hungary (2.5%). The only two non-European nationalities in this list were our neighbors, Canada and Mexico.

By 2015, Europeans accounted for only about 13 percent of immigrants. Latin America and Asia accounted for the ten largest U.S. immigrant groups: Mexico (26.9%), India (5.5%), China—not counting Hong Kong and Taiwan—(4.8%), Philippines (4.6%), El Salvador (3.1%), Vietnam (3.0%), Cuba (2.8%), Dominican Republic (2.5%), Korea (2.4%), and Guatemala (2.1%).[3]

In addition to a broadening of the nationality of immigrants, immigration rose to levels similar to those of the late 1800s and early 1900s (Figure 1). The foreign-born made up about 13.7 percent of the U.S. population in 2015, much higher than the 5.4 percent in 1960 and approaching the historically high 14.7 percent in 1910.[4] The children of all these new immigrants, even those born in the United States and thus citizens, became a focus of public discourse.

Keyword searches related specifically to "birthright citizenship" and "anchor babies" in articles of the *New York Times* and *Los Angeles Times* between 1965 and 2015 resulted in 308 news articles (stories that mentioned both birthright citizenship and anchor babies are listed under anchor baby stories).[5] These two newspapers serve as the nation's papers of record, and both cover politics and immigration extensively. Birthright citizenship became a "hot topic" in the 1990s and has continued apace (Figure 2). The term "anchor babies"

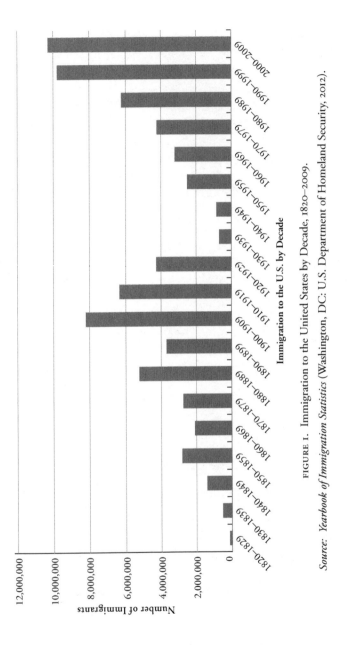

FIGURE 1. Immigration to the United States by Decade, 1820–2009.

Immigration to the U.S. by Decade

Source: *Yearbook of Immigration Statistics* (Washington, DC: U.S. Department of Homeland Security, 2012).

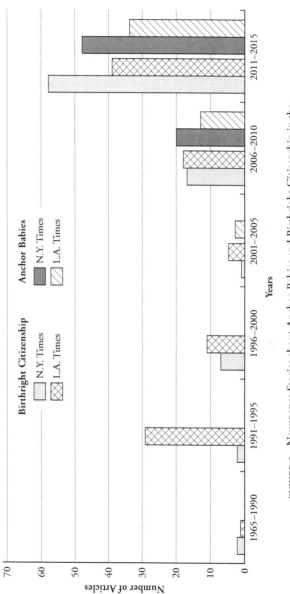

FIGURE 2. Newspaper Stories about Anchor Babies and Birthright Citizenship in the *New York Times* and *Los Angeles Times*, 1965–2015.

Source: Author's calculations of newspaper publications.

appeared in news stories in the early 2000s and surged as a media topic after 2005. So-called anchor babies were framed in negative terms, as underserving citizens out to cheat more deserving citizens. Just singling out a group of citizens as "anchor babies" called into question their citizenship, contributed to fearmongering, and fueled proposals to deny them birthright citizenship.

THE 1980S: ASSIMILATION AND CONSENT

The United States entered a major recession in the early 1980s. Immigration became a significant concern, and much of what appeared in the media was alarmist, suggesting America could not afford more immigration during a period of high unemployment. *U.S. News & World Report*'s April 12, 1982, cover asked, "Will U.S. Shut the Door on Immigrants?" Its March 7, 1983, cover had a photograph of a Mexican man carrying a woman across the Rio Grande into the United States, with the headline: "Invasion from Mexico: It Just Keeps Growing."[6] The image of the woman not so subtly suggested the "invasion" of fertile women who could have babies in the United States.

A *New York Times* headline on November 21, 1982, made this explicit: "Mexican Women Cross Border So Babies Can Be U.S. Citizens."[7] The article, set in Brownsville, Texas, across the border from Matamoros, Mexico, told the story of a 27-year-old woman who crossed the border legally to deliver her baby in Brownsville, "which is fairly typical of Mexican women, now numbering in the thousands, who are coming across the border every year to have their babies in the United States. They come, many of them, so the baby will be born an American citizen, with all the advantages that that brings."

A letter to the editor in the *New York Times* on January 13, 1983, expressed anger over the story of women crossing the border to have babies. The writer took issue with the idea that these babies will have the same rights and entitlements as other citizens, "including free public education, Social Security, Medicare, voting and the right to hold public office." Anger gave way to policy suggestions as the letter writer called for changing the Fourteenth Amendment and the principle of jus soli because "this principle is now being grossly and shamefully abused." Citizenship, he argued, should be denied if the baby's mother had not been in the United States for a reasonable amount of time and should be denied completely to the children of "illegal aliens." As the writer put it, "Congress should begin the process of altering the 14th Amendment so that its intent can no longer be so mischievously perverted."

In 1985, as the number of U.S.-born children with undocumented parents began to increase, two Yale University professors, Peter H. Schuck and Rogers M. Smith, raised the issue of birthright citizenship in their book *Citizenship without Consent: Illegal Aliens in the American Polity.*[8] They questioned granting birthright citizenship to the children of undocumented immigrants, arguing that the United States should move away from its principle of inclusion through birthright citizenship and replace it with citizenship by consent. The consent principle would make citizenship subject to consent, or agreement, by the nation and then, if granted, by the consent of those seeking citizenship upon reaching the age of legal majority.

Shuck and Smith's citizenship-through-consent proposal raises significant issues. U.S.-born children denied birthright citizenship could also be denied the opportunity of citizenship when they are older if the nation or state views them as a "threat" and decides to withhold consent. The consent principle for citizenship raises the possibility that nonconsent might also be applied to U.S.-born minorities, such as Muslims today, who are out of favor or stigmatized as a threat to the nation at a particular moment. U.S.-born noncitizens could also be deportable, as recently occurred in Germany.[9] In short, the principle of consent for citizenship could easily become a principle of exclusion. Finally, Schuck and Smith argued that the Fourteenth Amendment's clause, "subject to the jurisdiction thereof," applies only to legal immigrants and not to unauthorized immigrants.

At about the same time Shuck and Smith were questioning birthright citizenship, James O. Pace was pushing his self-published 1985 book, *Amendment to the Constitution*, in which he advocated repealing the Fourteenth Amendment.[10] Pace would deport or deny citizenship to everyone not of western European stock:

> No person shall be a citizen of the United States unless he is a non-Hispanic white of the European race, in whom there is no ascertainable trace of Negro blood, nor more than one-eighth Mongolian, Asian, Asia Minor, Middle Eastern, Semitic, Near Eastern, American Indian, Malay or other non-European or non-white blood, provided that Hispanic whites, defined as anyone with an Hispanic ancestor, may be citizens if, in addition to meeting the aforesaid ascertainable trace and percentage tests, they are in appearance indistinguishable from Americans whose ancestral home is in the British Isles or Northwestern Europe. Only citizens shall have the right and privilege to reside permanently in the United States.[11]

Although Pace's policy recommendations were outlandish in their breadth and call for race-based exclusions, they do show just how passionate, and fearful, some Americans were at the time about changing demographics and what they perceived as a dilution of their privileges as citizens. When Congress passed the Immigration Reform and Control Act of 1985 (IRCA), it included a significant increase in border controls and surveillance, employer sanctions, and an amnesty program for some undocumented immigrants. IRCA did not include anything dealing with birthright citizenship.

The fear that the children of Mexican immigrants would rather not assimilate, which would lead to a divided nation, was so prevalent at the time that *U.S. News & World Report*'s August 19, 1985, cover asked the question, "The Disappearing Border: Will the Mexican Migration Create a New Nation?" The magazine made clear that the threat to the United States was posed not just by immigrants but more profoundly by their children, even for generations:

> Now sounds the march of new conquistadors in the American Southwest. The heirs of Cortés and Coronado are rising again in the land their forebears took from the Indians and lost to the Americans. Their movement is, despite its quiet and largely peaceful nature, both an invasion and a revolt. At the vanguard are those born here, whose roots are generations deep, who long endured Anglo dominance and rule and who are ascending within the U.S. system to take power they consider their birthright.[12]

During this time, advocates for restrictive immigration policies focused on fertility of immigrant women and the fear of demographic change. In 1986, John Tanton wrote a memo he titled "The Latin Onslaught." Tanton, an ophthalmologist from Michigan, once president of Zero Population Growth and founder of the Federation for American Immigration Reform (FAIR), warned in his memo, "Will the present majority peaceably hand over its political power to a group (Latin American immigrants) that is simply more fertile? . . . On the demographic point: Perhaps this is the first instance in which those with their pants up are going to get caught by those with their pants down!"[13]

If the 1980s public discourse focused on the children of immigrants as a problem, public discourse and congressional bills in the 1990s repeatedly advocated for the solution: to eliminate or amend the Fourteenth Amendment's guarantee of birthright citizenship.

THE 1990S: THE BROWNING OF AMERICA

Beginning in 1990, the United States again was gripped by a major economic recession that held the nation at bay for the next few years. In California, the recession was exacerbated by withdrawal of federal funds for military bases and related programs. Two other issues contributed to the public's interest in immigration.

Undocumented immigration continued to grow, and demographic change was occurring such that European Americans were becoming a proportionately smaller part of the U.S. population.

In the late 1980s and early 1990s, demographic change became associated with the "browning of America." *Time* magazine's April 9, 1990, cover asked, "America's Changing Colors: What Will the U.S. Be Like When Whites Are No Longer the Majority?" *Time*'s answer: "The 'browning of America' will alter everything in society, from politics and education to industry, values and culture. . . . The deeper significance of America becoming a majority non-white society is what it means to the national psyche, to individuals' sense of themselves and the nation—their idea of what it is to be American."[14]

Time was prescient in its prediction that becoming a multiracial society will cause serious adjustment among whites, many of whom consider the nation as reflecting their own image. As *Time* put it:

> While know-nothingism is generally confined to the more dismal corners of the American psyche, it seems all too predictable that during the next decades many more mainstream white Americans will begin to speak openly about the nation they feel they are losing. There are not, after all, many non-white faces depicted in Norman Rockwell's paintings. White Americans are accustomed to thinking of themselves as the very picture of their nation.[15]

But what was perhaps a more telling link between immigrants and their children as posing future problems for the nation was the advertisement that accompanied *Time*'s April 9, 1990, issue. The image in the ad consisted of thirty-eight newborn babies arranged ten to a row, except for the bottom row, which had eight babies and a small copy of *Time*'s April 9, 1990, cover. The babies were a mix of various shades of brown. Only one baby, next to the cover's image, was white. The ad read: "Hey, whitey, your turn at the back of the bus. Sometime soon, white Americans will become a distinct minority in a largely brown cultural and racial mix."[16]

In October 1991, Representative Elton Gallegly (Rep. CA, Simi Valley) introduced legislation for a constitutional amendment that would deny citizenship to U.S.-born children with undocumented parents. Gallegly's argument in support of his bill stressed that it was both moral (deserving "American" children were being deprived) and economic (the cost of social services). "The bottom line, when you look at the cost for childbirth for children (for babies of illegal immigrants) and for payments to them afterward, is that all the other needy children . . . are being deprived."[17]

The response to Gallegly's bill for a constitutional amendment was swift. In October 1991, Latino leaders in Ventura County, California, "blasted" Gallegly's proposal, calling it "insulting, racist, mean-spirited and ill-conceived."[18] The following month, in November, a demonstration was held outside Gallegly's office in Chatsworth, California. In response to the demonstration, Gallegly reiterated his argument that government spending for the children of illegal immigrants in California is "bankrupting the state," an issue related to the deep recession at the time. He also argued that his bill would make the United States more like "every nation in the world" that has restrictions on citizenship and it would remove the lure of automatic citizenship to future immigrants. Demonstrators accused Gallegly of "trying to capitalize politically by falsely blaming U.S. economic problems on immigrants."[19]

Although Gallegly's proposal to deny citizenship to U.S.-born children gained little support among his colleagues, the publicity helped his reelection campaign that year. In December 1992, Representative Gallegly was appointed to the judiciary panel in the House of Representatives, where he could promote legislation to restrict immigration.[20]

Governor Pete Wilson was also a strong supporter of California's 1992 Proposition 187, which was to "Save Our State," in the words of its supporters, by denying "illegal aliens health care, education, and other publicly-funded benefits."[21] In reality, much of the concern among proponents of Proposition 187 had to do with pregnant immigrant mothers giving birth to U.S. citizens.[22] As Bette Hammond, organizer of California's Proposition 187, noted in 1994: "They come here, they have their babies, and after that they become citizens and all those children use social services."[23]

The following year, 1993, Governor Wilson continued the battle over birthright citizenship. In August, Wilson declared that California's recovery from recession was "under siege from illegal immigration." He proposed a wide range of solutions, including denying citizenship to children born in the United States to undocumented immigrants and cutting off their health and education benefits. Wilson argued the moral and economic benefits: "We do not exaggerate when we say that illegal immigration is eroding the quality of life for legal residents of California, is threatening the quality for education that we can provide our children, the quality of care to our needy and blind, elderly and disabled."[24] According to Wilson, ending birthright citizenship would end an important incentive that now entices immigrants to enter the United States illegally. "It is time to amend the Constitution so that citizenship belongs only to the children of legal residents of the United States, not to every child whose mother can make it to an American hospital."[25] Critics accused Wilson of being racially divisive and using nativist fears for his own political gain.

Those favoring Wilson's proposals to deny citizenship, education, and medical care to immigrants and their children agreed with his basic arguments. However, critics noted that migrants are typically lured to the United States to work and then later may form a family, rather than crossing the border to have a baby. Others emphasized that Canada, Mexico, and many Latin American countries confer birthright citizenship in contrast to Europe, where foreign laborers have slim or no prospects of becoming a citizen of their adopted countries. Wilson's proposals also faced a stiff challenge given that the U.S. Supreme Court's 1982 decision in *Plyler v. Doe* guaranteed education for immigrant children and that an amendment to the Constitution requires a two-thirds vote in both the House and Senate, plus ratification by 38 of the 50 states.[26] But the likelihood of such proposals actually being enacted may be less important than the symbolic benefits garnered by their proponents.

Given the obstacles to changing the Fourteenth Amendment, Governor Wilson focused on another strategy for reducing the number of U.S.-born children to undocumented mothers: cut off their access to prenatal and postnatal care programs, including education. Eventually, efforts to deny prenatal care to immigrant mothers, thus putting future U.S.-citizen babies at risk, were blocked in the courts. In November 1996, a California superior court judge blocked Governor Wilson's plan to cut off prenatal care to undocumented immigrants.[27]

The battle over birthright citizenship continued in the U.S. Congress. On August 4, 1993, Senator Harry Reid (Dem. NV) introduced the Immigration Stabilization Act of 1993.[28] In effect, the bill would have revoked birthright citizenship for children born in the United States to parents who are undocumented immigrants. In an August 5 memo, Reid argued that ending birthright citizenship would eliminate the "incentive for pregnant alien women to enter the United States illegally, often at the risk to mother and child, for the purpose of acquiring citizenship for the child and accompanying federal financial benefits."[29] The bill did not become law. Reid now calls the bill a "travesty," "a mistake," and the "low point" of his legislative career.[30]

In 1995, the House of Representatives considered a bill introduced by Republicans to amend the U.S. Constitution to end automatically granting citizenship to everyone born in the United States. Lawmakers from California, in particular, supported the bill, complaining that undocumented immigrants, mostly from Mexico, drained public services. Representative Brian P. Bilbray (Rep. CA, San Diego) complained of hospitals overcrowded with "illegal immigrant mothers who come to the United States to give birth. Once the children are born, they become United States citizens and the parents are, in effect, virtually immune from deportation."[31] Latino advocacy groups and the Clinton administration opposed the bill. Walter Dellinger, assistant attorney general and the Justice Department's chief constitutional scholar, warned the House panel discussing the bill that the proposal would alter how democracy is practiced in America by creating "a permanent caste of aliens, generation after generation, born in America but never to be among its citizens."[32]

Such concerns found a deaf ear at the 1996 Republican Convention. As the GOP's platform that year stated, "We support a constitutional amendment or constitutionally-valid legislation declaring that children born in the United States of parents who are not legally present in the United States or who are not long-term residents are not automatically citizens."[33] The proposal had its share of supporters, especially those concerned with the cost of social services and the alleged magnet of birthright citizenship to future immigrants. However, some within the GOP did not support the platform.[34] Senator Bob Dole (Rep. KS) stated in no uncertain terms that he did not support a constitutional amendment to deny automatic citizenship for children born in this country to undocumented parents.[35]

The GOP platform produced consternation in many quarters. As the *New York Times* noted, "In proposing to deny United States citizenship to children born in the country to illegal immigrants, members of the Republican Platform Committee are challenging a pillar of constitutional law erected nearly 130 years ago."[36] A. M. Rosenthal compared the GOP's platform to "Dred Scott," referring to the 1857 U.S. Supreme Court's infamous Dred Scott decision denying citizenship to African Americans born in the United States.[37] In addition, the *Los Angeles Times* noted that the Republican Party would have a problem attracting minorities, especially Latinos, because of the party's anti-immigration platform. It pointed specifically to the platform's call for amending the Constitution to deny citizenship to the children of undocumented immigrants.[38]

Despite the media attention and congressional hearings about changing the Fourteenth Amendment, the 1996 immigration law did not directly address the issue of birthright citizenship for the children of undocumented parents. The 1996 Illegal Immigration Reform and Immigration Responsibility Act toughened the requirements for undocumented immigrants to adjust their status to that of legal immigrant and streamlined the judicial process by turning deportation decisions over to an immigrant court, thereby reducing the level of judicial review available to immigrants. It also streamlined the deportation of criminals and expanded the range of deportable offenses. The immigration law indirectly, and perhaps unintentionally, dealt with the issue of U.S.-born children helping their parents to become legal residents of the United States by making the sponsors of those applying to become legal permanent residents economically responsible for public benefits used by those they sponsor. This economic burden added a major level of difficulty for low-income and even middle-income U.S. citizens who might desire to sponsor their undocumented parents and siblings.

A number of bills in Congress in 1997 dealt with birthright citizenship. The most significant of these bills perhaps was the Citizenship Reform Act of 1997, sponsored by Republican Brian Bilbray of San Diego. Critics argued that expansive U.S. citizenship laws differed from those in many other countries, underscoring the idea of U.S. exceptionalism.[39] Congressional hearings on the Citizenship Reform Act were highly contentious. Bilbray argued, "To claim that you can have a right of automatic citizenship is absurd. The Supreme Court has never ruled on the children of illegal aliens getting automatic citizenship." For Bilbray, granting citizenship rights is "rewarding those who have broken the law." A San Diego County supervisor testified, "We have encouraged generations of people to come to America, not out of loyalty or a sense of belonging, but instead, for money and benefits."[40] Those testifying against the bill focused on the constitutional guarantee of birthright citizenship. The acting assistant attorney general testified that the bill "is unquestionably unconstitutional."[41]

THE 2000S: HERE COME THE ANCHOR BABIES

The United States entered into the new millennium following an unprecedented period of economic growth in the second half of the 1990s. With low unemployment rates, falling fertility rates, and an aging population, the context was ripe for a demand of labor that was satisfied in part by undocumented workers.[42] So many undocumented workers were drawn to the United States during this time that they went from about 3 million in 1996 to about 8.8 million in 2000, and 10.3 million in 2004.[43] In addition, the expanding economy created a hyper-demand for foreign labor that pulled Mexican immigrants to "new" locations in the Midwest and southeastern United States.[44] Much of the migrant labor in the South was needed in chicken, beef, and pork production.[45] *The Nation*'s February 3, 1997, cover story addressed this new movement: "The Heartland's Raw Deal: How Meatpacking Is Creating a New Immigrant Underclass." The image was a man's body from the shoulders down, whose apron, gloves, and shoes were covered in blood. The image suggested the need for labor (body) but not necessarily for social beings (head).

The rapid growth of the Mexican immigrant population raised concerns. Samuel P. Huntington raised the alarm about Mexican immigration in *The American Enterprise* in 2000: "The invasion of over 1 million Mexican civilians is a comparable threat [as 1 million Mexican soldiers] to American societal security, and Americans should react against it with comparable vigor. Mexican immigration looms as a unique and disturbing challenge to our cultural integrity, our national identity, and potentially to our future as a country."[46]

The problem was that the longer they stayed, the more likely these new immigrant workers were to form families, or bring spouses and children to join them, contributing to demographic change and cultural change. *Time*'s June 11, 2001, issue featured two young Latino children, a girl and a boy, with the headline: "Welcome to Amexica: THE BORDER is vanishing before our eyes, creating a new world for all of us." The letters in the word "Amexica" were in colors taken from the Mexican and U.S. flags: *A* (red), *m* (white), *e* (blue), *x* (white), *i* (red), *c* (green), and *a* (white), to indicate both in colors and in the blending of the words "America" and "Mexico" that the two countries and people were becoming one.

While the children on the cover of *Time* seemed cute and part of a family that consumed the current fashions, they were anything but benign to those who considered children like them to be the vanguard of demographic change and a threat to the fiscal and cultural future of the United States. Without saying it, a reader could easily imagine that these were the anchor babies that would become such a prevalent part of public discourse.

After the September 11, 2001, terrorist attacks, the United States increasingly focused on the dangers of a hostile world. President George W. Bush developed a general strategy for the national security of the United States.[47] Meanwhile, nativism reared its ugly head as Arab Americans became prime targets of racial profiling and surveillance.[48] Americans seemed willing to allow the constitutional rights of foreigners and immigrants to become diminished so long as those of citizens remained intact, a dangerous bargain at best. Even three years later, *Time* magazine's September 20, 2004, issue focused on the porous U.S.-Mexico border as a security threat. The cover's image featured an American flag, the fabric of the nation, being torn apart by two brown (Latin

American?) hands. The headline read, "America's Borders: Even after 9/11 It's Outrageously Easy to Sneak In."

The new post–9/11 concerns for national security did not eclipse a public discourse on the alleged threat to the nation posed by Mexican immigration and the growing number of Americans of Mexican descent in the United States. However, the events of 9/11 "raised the stakes" and added a new and urgent argument for confronting all perceived threats to national security, both old and new. In 2004 Samuel Huntington showed that the threat posed by Mexican immigrants and their children still had currency in the new, post–9/11 world: "In this new era, the single most immediate and most serious challenge to America's traditional identity comes from the immense and continuing immigration from Latin America, especially from Mexico, and the fertility rates of those immigrants compared to black and white American natives."[49]

Linking Mexican immigration and fertility underscores the problem of children as part of a foreign "invasion" or "reconquest." This threat, for some, was great enough that they were willing to jettison the constitutional guarantee of citizenship by birth for all children born in the United States.

In 2001, Glenn Spencer, with his organization Voice of Citizens Together, voiced what would soon become his post–9/11 concerns.[50] Spencer's crusade was against what he called Mexico's *Reconquista* of California and the Southwest, relaxed borders, and free trade. "The 'invasion' of poor Mexicans and Central Americans was costing Americans jobs, dragging down public schools, despoiling the environment, spreading disease and exacerbating sundry other social problems." He waged his battle on the Internet and on a privately financed radio program (called "American Patrol") to warn against Mexico's "demographic war" against the United States. As he put it: "We are faced, as I've said for 10 years now, with the greatest threat to the security of the United States in our history. We're being invaded ladies and gentlemen. We're making it easier and easier for people from the entire planet to come here and colonize us and take away our nation."[51]

The threat, for Spencer, was both cultural and demographic. Spencer did not believe the children of Mexican and Central American immigrants are integrating into U.S. life and culture. Rather, they "are remaining separate by choice. Their culture is maintained, as is their language." Birthright citizenship, according to Spencer, was allowing the reconquest to occur: "Now all a Mexican has to do is have a baby, and she and her boyfriend are set for life. Scavenging for work on street corners, or selling dope to U.S. teenagers, helps supplement free giveaways from the Yankee suckers."[52] Here we have both the moral argument (notice the woman is not married and is a drug pusher) and the economic argument (a taker of giveaways, which is a way of saying social services).

In the mid-2000s, Lou Dobbs used his CNN television program to help make "anchor babies" a household word. Through almost weekly stories, Dobbs emphasized the threat posed by anchor babies as part of a plot by their parents to gain U.S. citizenship. As Dobbs explained in April 2006: "Tonight the fight is on in Congress over so-called anchor babies. Some 200,000 anchor babies are born to illegal aliens in this country each year. These babies instantly become U.S. citizens, and illegal alien parents of anchor babies can become citizens as well with the sponsorship of those babies as they grow up. Many in Congress, in increasing numbers, now say those birthright protections simply have to end."[53]

Latin Americans were not the only ones accused of taking advantage of birthright citizenship. Thousands of South Korean parents (up to five thousand Korean babies a year by one estimate) were coming to the United States to have a U.S.-citizen baby. These "birth tourists" were often better-off South Koreans, willing to pay up to $20,000 for advantages of U.S. citizenship, especially American schools, and to avoid serving in the South Korean military. The practice, however, is not illegal so long as parents can afford the medical bills. Critics, such as the Federation for American Immigration Reform (FAIR), called these children "anchor babies." "It is hard to conceptualize a strategy that is so long-term (21 years) with regard to U.S. citizenship, but that is what they are doing—establishing a foothold."[54]

Affluent Mexicans living in Mexican border cities like Tijuana also sometimes cross the border to have babies that are U.S. citizens.[55] If they are able to prove financial stability and their place of permanent residence, Mexicans can obtain a visitor's visa that allows travel 25 miles from the border for up to three days. With the ability to pay for medical care, they are often sought after by medical providers on the U.S. side of the border. Critics claim that providers are taking advantage of wealthy women being able to have their babies in the United States. In 2003, Barbara Coe, who headed the California Coalition for Immigration Reform in Orange County, called these children "anchor babies." "Because they are born here they end up funding the needs for the entire illegal alien family. It's a tremendous welcome mat for illegal aliens."[56]

The children of immigrants were also said to be "changing the face of New York's neighborhoods." Since 1990, the number of Mexican immigrants, about 80–85 percent undocumented, had quadrupled. Mexican-born mothers gave birth to 6,408 babies in 2000, second only to foreign-born Dominicans (births to Mexican women would surpass births to Dominican-born women in 2005).[57] Overall, immigration had economic benefits to the city. According to the director of the City Planning Department, "If we didn't have immigration, I don't know where we'd be. Immigrant flows have mitigated catastrophic population losses in the 1970s, stabilized the city's population in the 1980's, and helped the city reach a new population peak of over 8 million in 2000."[58]

On February 9, Representative Nathan Deal (Rep. GA) introduced the Citizenship Reform Act of 2005. The bill proposed to amend the Immigration and Nationality Act to limit automatic citizenship at birth to a child born in the United States who (1) "was born in wedlock to a parent either of whom is a U.S. citizen or national, or is an alien lawfully admitted for permanent residence who maintains his or her residence in the United States," or (2) "was born out of wedlock to a mother who is a U.S. citizen or national, or is an alien lawfully admitted for permanent residence who maintains his or her residence in the United States."[59]

Deal's bill to change the Fourteenth Amendment had the support of the 92-member House Immigration Reform Caucus, headed by Tom Tancredo (Rep. CO). As Representative Lamar Smith (Rep. TX) argued: "Illegal immigrants are coming for many different reasons. Some are coming for jobs. Some are coming to give birth. Some are coming to commit crimes. Addressing this problem is needed if we're going to combat illegal immigration on all fronts." Again, supporters focused on the phrase "subject to the jurisdiction thereof" in the Fourteenth Amendment as not applying to parents living in the country illegally. Critics noted that there was no evidence that removing birthright citizenship would significantly affect undocumented immigration, yet it would create a population of "stateless" children.[60] The bill would ultimately go nowhere, leading Representative Deal to reintroduce the bill in 2007 and in 2009, both of which were also unsuccessful.

Women migrating to the United States on their own added to concerns over anchor babies.[61] A story in the *New York Times* in 2006 focused on a young woman who migrated without documentation to work in a Kansas meatpacking plant for $15 an hour. "A growing number of single women . . . are coming not to join husbands, but to find jobs, send money home and escape a bleak future in Mexico. They come to find work in the booming underground economy, through a vast network of friends and relatives already employed here as maids, cooks, kitchen helpers, factory workers and baby sitters. In these jobs, they can earn double or triple their Mexican salaries."[62] With more women migrants comes increased concern over the cost to hospitals for births and the use of social services, especially schools. Immigrant advocates, however, argue that "the women's reasons for coming here reach far beyond citizenship for their children; few women come to the United States expressly to have babies, collect benefits and visit the emergency room."[63]

The increase in women migrating to the United States coincided with an upswing in anger over undocumented immigration. On December 15, 2005, the House of Representatives passed HR 4437, the Border Protection, Antiterrorism, and Illegal Immigration Control Act. Although it never became law, it raised fears among immigrants and their families and led to major marches for immigrant rights throughout the United States in 2006.[64] HR 4437 had many draconian provisions, but one of the most feared among immigrant families made living in the United States as an undocumented immigrant a felony, thus removing any hope of someday becoming a legal permanent resident. In addition, there were stiff penalties for transporting and harboring undocumented immigrants and assisting them to live in the United States. The bill's provisions were so broad that even U.S.-born children could have been held accountable for helping their undocumented parents.

Texas was an example of a state grappling with ways to deal with immigration. One key issue was the cost of medical care, especially for pregnancy and delivery of babies. Two Texas hospitals offered a contrast in their approach. One hospital welcomed immigrant women, and one hospital demanded some form of identification to show that the person was legally in the country.[65] The two approaches reflected the public's divergent attitudes. Texas has its share of anti-immigrant sentiment: "We have a lot of United States citizens that need our help in health, and we should pull them up before we pull up someone here illegally." Many Texans favor deporting undocumented women who seek care from public hospitals, even if they give birth to an American citizen. On the other hand, the director of the Texas hospital association noted that "While Texas border hospitals often get 'anchor babies'—children of Mexican women who dart across the border to give birth to an American citizen—most illegal immigrants who go to major hospitals in Texas can show that they have been living here for years."[66]

Pearson, Georgia, served as an example of a small town coping with newcomers. Mexican immigrants began arriving in Pearson in the 1990s, lured by jobs in agriculture and manufacturing. With one traffic light, and mostly white or black residents, Pearson's Mexicans stood out. Suddenly, locals felt dislocated as their community's ethnic identity underwent change. One resident expressed his fear: "The way the Mexicans have children, they're going to have a majority here soon. I have children and grandchildren. They're going to become second-class citizens. And we're going to be a third world country here if we don't do something about it." Meanwhile, the Mexicans in Pearson were setting down roots and felt both pride at what they had accomplished and alienation because of the town's ambivalence toward them. As one woman, who was 12 when she came from Mexico, put it: "I call it home, but I know I'm not welcome in my own home. Maybe that feeling of home will be something that will always be missing for me."[67]

The issue of anchor babies complicated even a national toy store's well-meaning sweepstakes. Toys "R" Us quickly found itself in a publicity nightmare when it tried to determine the winner of its national sweepstakes for the first American baby born in 2007. The prize was a $25,000 U.S. savings bond. A baby girl, Yuki Lin, was born just as the last ball in Times Square fell. However, Toys "R" Us ruled her ineligible because her mother was not a legal resident of the United States. In her place, Toys "R" Us awarded the savings bond to a baby born to an African American. The Chinese American community and the Chinese business community were outraged and complained loudly. As a leader of a Chinese American organization put it: "I am strongly opposed to the Toys 'R' Us decision to give the award to another baby just based solely on the mother's status. . . . Anyone who is here should be protected by law—especially a baby with the same rights as any other citizen." Critics suggested that had the company not made this decision, it might have faced problems from those against "anchor babies."[68]

The story of Henry Cejudo, who earned a gold medal in wrestling in the Beijing Summer Olympics, exemplifies how the anchor baby controversy can taint accomplishments otherwise worthy of national pride. Cejudo was born in Los Angeles to undocumented parents from Mexico. With a deadbeat dad, he was raised by his mother in cities around the Southwest. Poor, angry, and hanging out with the wrong crowd, Henry was fortunate to turn his energy to wrestling. At 21, Henry was the youngest American to win a freestyle wrestling gold medal. After winning, he said: "I'm living the American dream. The United States is the land of opportunity, and I'm so glad I can represent it."[69] However, the heated politics over anchor babies made it difficult for some to see Henry Cejudo as an American hero, as this letter to the editor of the *Los Angeles Times* indicated: "Some may see him as a gold medalist, but a majority of Americans will always see him and his five siblings as anchor babies."[70]

Among those calling for a reexamination of the Fourteenth Amendment in 2010 were many Republican congressional leaders, including Mitch McConnell, John McCain, Lindsey Graham, Jeff Sessions, and Jon Kyl. Graham was most emphatic, claiming it was a "mistake" to grant birthright citizenship to the children of undocumented immigrants. "We can't just have people swimming across the river having children here—that's chaos."[71] Lamar Smith of Texas and Steve King of Iowa both thought denying birthright citizenship to "anchor babies" was a good idea. King, a staunch supporter of Arizona's harsh immigration laws and defender of racial profiling, at one time even proposed putting electrified wire on the border as done for livestock.[72] Representative Duncan Hunter (Rep. CA) told a Tea Party rally in California that the children of undocumented immigrants should be deported, even if they are U.S. citizens. "It takes more than walking across the border to become an American citizen."[73] Of course, the babies did not walk across the border; the mother did at some point in her life. In an editorial, the *New York Times* called proposals to change the Fourteenth Amendment "fear-mongering for American votes" and argued that the Fourteenth Amendment "cannot fall prey to political whims or debates over who is worthy to be an American."[74]

Citing federal inaction on immigration, states took up the battle over birthright citizenship. An oft-repeated concern was the cost borne by states of social services for the children of undocumented immigrants, and the lure of citizenship for undocumented immigrants.[75] On April 23, 2010, Arizona governor Jan Brewer signed into law Senate Bill 1070, the Support Our Law and Safe Neighborhoods Act.[76] SB 1070 had a number of harsh provisions, including that immigrants must have their documents in their possession at all times, and that law enforcement was required to attempt to determine an individual's immigration status when stopped, detained, or arrested, if there was a reasonable suspicion of the person's status. "Reasonable suspicion" was vague and critics viewed it as giving the police broad powers. The goal of such provisions was making life so tough on undocumented families that there would be "attrition through enforcement." Arizona state senator Russell Pearce, author of SB 1070, believed the law did not go far enough, and he said he would push to deny U.S. citizenship to children born in Arizona to undocumented parents.[77]

Although much of Arizona's SB 1070 would be ruled unconstitutional, it spurred other states to consider or pass harsh immigration-related laws. Republicans were also emboldened by huge midterm election gains (690 seats) in state legislatures nationwide. In late 2010, at least six states—Georgia, Mississippi, Nebraska, Oklahoma, Pennsylvania, and South Carolina—indicated they would form a coordinated effort to cancel automatic citizenship for the children born in the United States to undocumented parents. Daryl Metcalfe, a Republican state representative from Pennsylvania, said his goal was to eliminate "an anchor baby status, in which an illegal alien invader comes into our country and has a child on our soil that is granted citizenship automatically."[78] Some Republicans, however, worried that such drastic proposals would lose Latino voters, an essential constituency given their growing political clout.

At about this time, Senator Lindsey Graham provided one of the most egregious arguments for questioning whether so-called anchor babies were deserving of citizenship. Appearing on Fox News on July 28, 2010, Graham said: "People come here to have babies. They come here to drop a child. It's called drop and leave. To have a child in America, they cross the border, they go to the emergency room, they have a child, and that child's automatically an American citizen. That shouldn't be the case. That attracts people for all the wrong reasons."[79] Graham used an animal metaphor when characterizing undocumented mothers as coming "to drop" a child. In English, we speak of animals—cats, horses, cows, and so on—as dropping their litter, foal, calf, and so on. Humans give birth. In Spanish, it is said women "give light" (*dar la luz*) to the baby by bringing it into the world. By using an animal metaphor, Graham both dismissed the women's humanity and underscored their threat to the United States by having babies that are part of a conspiracy to circumvent the nation's immigration laws.[80]

Shortly thereafter, Peter Schuck argued that Congress could alter the Fourteenth Amendment without a constitutional amendment. Congress, in his view, could put conditions on citizenship, such as only after a certain number of years in American schools, for the children of undocumented immigrants, who could then apply for citizenship at, say, age ten or older. This would indicate a genuine connection to American society.[81]

Gregory Rodriguez, the filmmaker, responded to Schuck. Rodriguez argued that a genuine connection to society is important, but it is birthright citizenship that promotes such a connection by creating reciprocal obligations. He argued that rather than creating a caste of stateless and permanent outsiders of native-born noncitizens, "it is in this country's best interest to absorb the children of those who have made their way here and thereby to establish the reciprocal obligations of citizenship . . . American history has proved that the broader our sense of civic inclusion, the stronger our nation. The Republican Party's search for enemies will only make us weaker."[82] The stateless caste Rodriguez referred to are those children who, for whatever reason, cannot make the transition to citizenship after being born in the United States.

2010S: THE ANCHOR BABY NARRATIVE GOES VIRAL

The *New York Times*' prescient January 4, 2011, headline read, "Birthright Citizenship Looms as Next Immigration Battle."[83] In 2011, conservative pundit Patrick J. Buchanan published his third book warning of the perils of immigration: *Suicide of a Superpower: Will America Survive to 2025?* According to Buchanan, "The erroneous interpretation of the Fourteenth Amendment that any child born to an illegal alien is automatically a U.S. citizen should be corrected by Congress via a provision attached to the law that is not subject to review by a federal court, including the U.S. Supreme Court."[84] Such action is needed, he argued, because the children of Mexican immigrants, even three generations later, do not assimilate and do not identify as Americans.[85] Buchanan is convinced that these children and even grandchildren, U.S. citizens by birth, will carry out the reconquest of California and the Southwest: "*La Reconquista* is not to be accomplished by force of arms, as was the U.S. annexation of the Southwest and California in 1848. It is to be carried out by a nonviolent invasion and cultural transformation of that huge slice of America into a Mexamerican borderland."[86]

Just five days into 2011, five conservative legislators from Arizona, Georgia, Oklahoma, Pennsylvania, and South Carolina held a news conference in Washington, DC, to talk about two bills they introduced into their state legislatures that would deny citizenship rights to the children of undocumented immigrants.[87] This was also the first day of the Republican-controlled 112th Congress. Daryl Metcalfe, a Republican state representative from Pennsylvania, explained the group's actions: "We are here to send a very public message to Congress. We want to bring an end to the illegal alien invasion that is having such a negative impact on our states."[88] The first bill would create state citizenship, which would be denied to babies born with two undocumented parents. The second bill would create special birth certificates that would be issued by all five states to babies whose parents could not prove that they were legal residents of the United States. Babies of immigrants living legally in the country on temporary visas would also be denied citizenship. The state legislators did not explain how their bills would work given the Fourteenth Amendment's clear statement about the citizenship of those born in the nation. Critics worried that these bills "will not drive away illegal immigrants [who come to work], but . . . would turn generations of young Americans into deportable criminals."[89]

As his first act in the new Congress, Representative Steve King (Rep. IA) also introduced the Birthright Citizenship Act of 2011. King's bill proposed changing the definition of "under the jurisdiction thereof" to qualify for citizenship so that it did not include undocumented immigrants. A child born in the United States would acquire birthright citizenship if one of its parents were a citizen or national of the United States; an alien lawfully admitted for permanent residence in the United States whose residence is the United States; or an alien performing active service in the armed forces. In other words, babies whose two parents were undocumented immigrants, or could not prove they qualified for one of the three provisions, would not acquire birthright citizenship. The bill did not clarify what status, rights, and responsibilities would befall the children who were U.S.-born noncitizens. Nor did it clarify how they would be identified, nor any actions or nonactions to be taken by government authorities toward these newborns. While the law would produce a new category of people—U.S.-born noncitizens—it did not consider the legal and social implications, intended or unintended, of the law.

Birth tourism, or the "maternity tourist," was again in the news in 2011. In San Gabriel, California, officials raided a row of connected townhouses occupied by relatively wealthy Chinese women and their newborn babies, who were new American citizens.[90] The women were legally in the United States on tourist visas. A similar operation appeared in Queens, New York.[91] Mark Krikorian, executive director of the Center for Immigration Studies and advocate for restrictive immigration laws, noted that most of the women and their babies return to China: "But if anything, it is worse than illegal immigrants delivering a baby here. Those kids are socialized as Americans. This phenomenon of coming to the U.S. and then leaving with people who have unlimited access to come back is just ridiculous."[92] Given such numbers, the vice president for immigration policy and advocacy at the Center for American Progress said: "I think it deserves a lot more study and a lot more attention. But to say that you want to change the Constitution because of this feels like killing a fly with an Uzi."[93] This complex issue will surface again.

Two demographic stories were related to the anchor baby controversy. First, the Pew Hispanic Center reported that the Mexican-origin population is growing more from births than from immigration.[94] From 2000 to 2010, about 7.2 million babies were born to mothers of Mexican origin in the United States. In 2010, about 227,500 children were born to at least one undocumented immigrant. For some people, these statistics add fuel to concerns of a demographic reconquest. But the second report may have dampened such fears. Between 2007 and 2010, Latinas, both immigrant and native born, had steeper declines in births than did other groups. Mexican American women had the steepest declines in birthrates. As William H. Frey, demographer at the Brookings Institution, noted: "It is surprising. When you hear about a decrease in the birthrate, you don't expect Latinos to be at the forefront of the trend."[95]

The battle over anchor babies and birthright citizenship really heated up in 2015, as the race for president of the United States got under way. Donald Trump's presidential campaign, in particular, ratcheted up the anchor baby issue and nativist views on immigration, in general. As the *New York Times* put it: "It has long been a hard job to keep the highly combustible immigration debate on the right side of sanity and reality. That progress is now being undone before our eyes in the presidential campaign, courtesy of the faux-populist billionaire who says immigrants are the reason this country is weak and frightened and going to hell."[96]

On Sunday, August 16, 2015, Donald Trump discussed the outline of his immigration policy on his webpage and on *Meet the Press*. His plan is to build a "huge" wall, strengthening border enforcement, and deporting all the "illegal aliens" in the country. Mr. Trump's proposals take little heed of the mixed status of so-called immigrant families. For Mr. Trump, deporting U.S.-born children along with their parents is not a problem: "We have to keep families together, but they have to go."[97] Limiting U.S. citizenship is part of Trump's plan for controlling immigration. Trump has said he would end birthright citizenship for children of parents living illegally inside the United States. "They have to go. What they are doing, they're having a baby. And then all of a sudden, nobody knows. . . . The baby's here." Even though they are U.S. born, "They're illegal. You either have a country or not."[98]

Donald Trump's inflammatory comments and proposals ignited a firestorm on the campaign trail, in the media, and in the blogosphere.[99] In short, Trump set the agenda on immigration for the Republican primary season. All candidates were questioned about their positions on immigration vis-à-vis Trump's proposals. Some Republican candidates toughened their stance on immigration, such as Governor Scott Walker of Wisconsin, Rick Santorum, Senator Rand Paul of Kentucky, Ben Carson, Governor Chris

Christie of New Jersey, and Bobby Jindal of Louisiana, a birth-right citizen himself.[100] Others already agreed with the idea of ending birthright citizenship, such as Ted Cruz of Texas. But others, such as Jeb Bush of Florida, Marco Rubio of Florida, Rick Perry of Texas, and Carly Fiorina of California, found such a proposal too harsh and a problem for attracting Latinos to the Republican Party.[101] Jeb Bush made his position clear on the issue of citizenship: "The courts have ruled that it's part of 14th Amendment of our Constitution and my belief is that it ought to stay that way, that this is part of our noble heritage."[102]

Use of the term "anchor baby" became a major point of contention. Donald Trump used the term often, even when told that it was offensive. "People like to say 'undocumented' because it's politically correct. I'll use the word 'anchor baby.'"[103] While many have come to expect such use of inflammatory and derogatory language from Trump, when Jeb Bush used "anchor baby" it drew a quick response from critics. Hillary Clinton tweeted, "They're called babies."[104]

But what really put Bush into hot water was his defense of his use of the term "anchor babies." He said people needed to "chill out" when it comes to political correctness, and besides it was "ludicrous" to suggest he was saying something negative about Hispanics. He explained that when he used the term "anchor babies" he was referring to people from Asian countries that sneak into the United States to have babies. "I was talking about a very narrow casted system of fraud, where people are bringing pregnant women in to have babies, to give birthright citizenship." The response from Asian Americans was quick. Representative Judy Chu (Dem. CA) responded: "No matter which ethnic group you're referring to, 'anchor babies' is a slur that stigmatizes children from birth. All that is accomplished through talk of anchor babies—be they from Latin America, Asia, Europe or Africa—is to use xenophobic fears to further isolate immigrants."[105]

Critics admonished Jeb Bush for his gaffe, noting that it was unnecessary because Mr. Trump and the anti-immigration crowd do not really use the term for "maternity tourism," which is a separate and much smaller issue. As the *New York Times* put it: "When they say 'anchor babies,' they are talking about the browning of America, with its growing Latino population, and recasting it as a sinister plot by child-rearing Mexicans. They want to upend the 14th amendment, and the country's family-based immigration laws, to keep the population as white as can be."[106]

Throughout 2015 and 2016, immigration and anchor babies were hot-button issues. Trump's incendiary comments on Mexicans, Muslims, African Americans and crime, and on women resulted in much polarization and fears among moderate Republicans about the future of the party, especially its relationship with Latinos.[107] Rallies and demonstrations both for and against Donald Trump's inflammatory positions on immigration occurred wherever he spoke, sometimes turning violent.[108] All of this social turmoil occurred quite apart from a rational debate over the country's future immigration policies.[109] Ultimately, Donald Trump's hard stance on immigration, including his focus on anchor babies, propelled him to the presidency in 2016.

Since assuming the presidency, Trump has made immigration a number-one priority, with executive actions limiting entry of refugees and immigrants from predominantly Muslim countries and broadening the grounds for deportation to include anyone who is in the country without authorization. In addition, Stephen Bannon and Steve Miller, two of his top aides, along with Jeff Sessions, the U.S. attorney general, are strong advocates for restricting immigration, both undocumented and legal, in favor of European immigration as a way of returning the country to an earlier demographic profile. In 2015, Jeff Session said the 1924 immigration national origin quotas, which barred most Asians, Italians, Jews, Africans, Middle Easterners, and other southern and eastern Europeans, "was good for America."[110]

Representative Steve King (Rep. IA), a longtime supporter of removing the Fourteenth Amendment for so-called anchor babies, reintroduced the Birthright Citizenship Act (HR 140) in early January 2017 to end birthright citizenship for children born in the United States to undocumented immigrants. King said: "A Century ago, it didn't matter very much that a single practice began that has now grown into a massive issue of birthright citizenship or the anchor baby agenda. When automatic citizenship started being granted to all babies born in the United States, our lawmakers missed the clause in the 14th Amendment that says, 'And subject to the jurisdiction thereof.'"[111] King ratcheted up his rhetoric of the threat posed by the children of today's non-European immigrants in the decline of "American culture." On May 12, 2017, he tweeted that "culture and demographics are our destiny. We can't restore our civilization with somebody else's babies."[112]

Shortly after assuming the presidency, Trump appointed Jon D. Feere, an outspoken critic of undocumented immigration, to the Department of Homeland Security. Feere is a legal policy analyst at the Center for Immigration Studies, which promotes restrictive immigration policies, and he has advocated ending birthright citizenship.[113] Trump's harsh rhetoric and actions toward immigrants and their children has emboldened many. "Reinvigorated" by Donald Trump's election, a nonprofit group, American Children First, began a petition in April 2017 in San Bernardino County, California, to ban undocumented students from schools, and to charge U.S.-born children of undocumented immigrants nonresident tuition.[114]

Such comments reflect a widening gap in views between the nation's two major political parties. In 2016, 60 percent of Americans opposed getting rid of birthright citizenship. However, a majority of Republicans (53%) favored changing the Constitution to ban birthright citizenship, compared to an overwhelming majority of Democrats (75%) opposed to any change.[115] Such polls reflect the conflicting nature of American attitudes toward immigration and the difficulty of making changes to the U.S. Constitution.

What is gained by keeping the debate on anchor babies and birthright citizenship alive? It keeps the issue in the public's imagination. Although proponents of changing or amending the Fourteenth Amendment to solve the anchor baby "problem" have yet to find legislative success, the very fact that there was a highly public discourse on anchor babies and birthright citizenship over decades framed the way this specific group of American citizens was being characterized and defined in the public's imagination. The question that emerges is whether or not *these* children are citizens like the rest of us.

It is in this sense that we speak of discourse being productive.[116] The news stories we constantly consume not only inform us of life around us but also help construct our understanding of events, people, and places in our world.[117] Public discourse about anchor babies and birthright citizenship help define what it means to be a "deserving citizen," a task that can be undertaken only by also constructing its opposite, the "underserving citizen."[118]

The public discourse over anchor babies and birthright citizenship, whether at the national level or in local towns and cities across the nation, produces people we can now talk about as "suspect citizens." As suspect citizens, anchor babies were, and are, subject to a set of negative characterizations that make them into a threat to the nation: their parents broke the law to come here, and so the very act of being born on U.S. soil is unacceptable, rendering these children undeserving of citizenship; they only take social benefits rather than give their loyalty to and produce value for this country; and they are part of their parents' conspiracy to take advantage of the United States by having a U.S.-citizen baby that can help them become legal residents of this country someday. For some, these children are also the harbingers of demographic change and cultural decline. Attempts to rebuke such characterizations actually have the effect of keeping them alive in public talk. Such rhetoric sends the message that *these* children *are* different from other citizens.

What is missing from much of the public discourse on anchor babies is a sense of how citizenship has been historically constructed. Why did the framers of the Fourteenth Amendment of the U.S. Constitution find it necessary to define who deserves to be a citizen? How did the U.S.-born children of immigrants complicate the definition of citizenship? Did a parent's immigration status disqualify the child from citizenship? The Fourteenth Amendment talks about being "under the jurisdiction thereof" of the United States, an issue often raised in current public discourse over anchor babies. But what has that jurisdictional issue meant historically when it comes to the children of immigrants?

2 A HISTORY OF BIRTHRIGHT CITIZENSHIP

How have changes in legal definitions of citizenship affected the children of immigrants? To answer this question, and to more fully understand the present controversy over anchor babies, we need to return to the beginning, to the thirteen English colonies along the eastern seaboard of North America. At the time, British law recognized that children in the colonies born to subjects of the Crown were themselves "natural born" subjects of the crown.[1] After separating from Britain, the new United States Constitution continued the idea of a natural-born citizen for the purposes of the presidency. Although not defined by the Constitution, a natural-born citizen is generally defined as a person born on U.S. territory. A person born abroad to a U.S. citizen father (later changed to include mothers) would be considered natural born for the purpose of being eligible for president. The Naturalization Act of 1790 affirmed the natural-born definition for those children born abroad, so long as the parent(s) had been resident in the United States at some point.[2]

The framers of the Constitution believed that having the natural-born citizen requirement for president would prevent a foreign-born president having divided loyalty between the United States and the president's country of birth. They believed a president's sole loyalty should be to the United States, with little opportunity for intrigue on behalf of foreign governments and, as commander in chief, for purposes of war.[3]

While the legal definition of natural-born citizen was important for the presidency, citizenship itself was broader. Two principles underlay citizenship in the United States, then and now. The first principle is *jus sanguinis* (Latin for "right of blood"). Jus sanguinis determines citizenship through parentage, in which one or both parents are citizens of the state. Simply put, having a father or mother (this varies by country) who is a citizen confers citizenship on the child.

The second principle is known as *jus soli*, which allows citizenship as a result of being born in the nation's territory. The word "nation" is derived from *nascere*, "to be born." This born-into-nation idea, jus soli, is the basis for the United States conferring birthright citizenship on those born inside its borders. The principle of jus soli is inclusive in that it allows anyone to become a member of the community of citizens simply through birth; citizenship is thus a right of birth, or birthright. Combing jus soli and jus sanguinis in this way made the United States different from many nations, past and present, that relied only on blood descent through the father (very typical), mother (less typical), or both to determine membership in the nation.

In an 1829 treatise on the U.S. Constitution, William Rawle, a prominent Philadelphia lawyer and onetime U.S. district attorney, wrote that "every person born within the United States, its territories or districts, whether the parents are citizens or aliens, is a natural born citizen in the sense of the Constitution, and entitled to all the rights and privileges appertaining to that capacity."[4] Similarly, in an 1830 case to settle the disposition of the estate of a man born in New York in 1776, the U.S. Supreme Court found that since the man was born when the Americans had jurisdiction over the city, he was a U.S. citizen. The court held: "Nothing is better settled at the common law than the doctrine that the children even of aliens born in a country while the parents are resident there under the protection of the government and owing a temporary allegiance thereto are subjects by birth."[5]

On March 30, 1854, the Honorable William L. Marcy, secretary of state, used similar logic to explain the status of the children of immigrants in a *New York Times* article titled "Native Sons of Alien Parents." He began by acknowledging that at the time the courts had yet to decide the issue of natural-born citizen. But he noted:

> I am under the impression that every person born in the United States must be considered a citizen, notwithstanding one—or both of his parents may have been alien at the time of his birth. This is in conformity with the English Common Law, which law is generally acknowledged in this country; and a person born of alien parents would, it is presumed, be considered such natural born citizen, in the language of the Constitution, as to make him eligible to the Presidency.[6]

Today, jus soli is more common in countries that have historically been settled by immigrants,[7] where birthright citizenship was useful in integrating immigrants of diverse origins into the nation.[8] Some countries do not confer citizenship automatically at birth but later on, after some criterion is met, such as when persons turn a specific age or exhibit certain criteria of deservingness (such as speaking the national language or living in the country for a set number of years) to show they have earned membership in the nation.[9]

For other nations where blood, race, and nation remain closely linked in terms of ethnic identity and national membership, jus sanguinis is often the preferred way to determine citizenship.[10] And a country's preference for citizenship by birth or by blood can change. Germany recently changed from jus sanguinis to a modified jus soli. In Ireland, as African refugees have increasingly settled in the country, a contentious referendum was passed in 2004, shifting from birthright citizenship to a more restrictive policy.[11]

The principle of citizenship through birth was common law and practice in the early U.S. republic, at least for "free white people."

As the Naturalization Act of 1790 made clear, naturalization was reserved for "free white person(s)" with at least two years residence in the United States. Birthright citizenship was not generally applied to babies born to nonwhites. Native Americans, the descendants of African slaves, and the children of Asian immigrants were generally not included as citizens in the country of their birth before the Fourteenth Amendment to the U.S. Constitution.

An anomaly were persons of Mexican descent, who were generally not considered "white" but suddenly found themselves living in territory ceded to the United States as a result of the war with Mexico (1846–48).[12] As a condition for signing the Treaty of Guadalupe Hidalgo, Mexico insisted that the Mexicans in the ceded territory be guaranteed U.S. citizenship with full civil rights.[13] Mexican settlers could use the treaty to request naturalization despite the "whites only" requirement at the time.[14]

THE FOURTEENTH AMENDMENT

After the Civil War, the Fourteenth Amendment made citizenship through birth the law of the land. Based on the principle of jus soli, U.S. citizenship is automatically conferred on any baby born in the United States. As Section 1 of the Fourteenth Amendment to the U.S. Constitution, adopted in 1868, states:

> All persons born or naturalized in the United States, and subject to the jurisdiction thereof, are citizens of the United States and of the State wherein they reside. No State shall make or enforce any law which shall abridge the privileges or immunities of citizens of the United States; nor shall any State deprive any person of life, liberty, or property, without due process of law; nor deny to any person within its jurisdiction the equal protection of the laws.[15]

The Fourteenth Amendment guaranteed citizenship to African Americans, who had routinely been excluded from citizenship even though they were born on U.S. soil. However, the Fourteenth

Amendment and birthright citizenship required further clarification in a nation that was multiracial. The case of the Chinese and their children, in particular, became a constitutional issue that has had repercussions for all future immigrants and their children.

The Chinese began migrating to the United States in significant numbers in the 1850s. Anti-Chinese nativism in the 1800s was virulent, culminating in the Chinese Exclusion Act of 1882, which effectively barred Chinese immigration and naturalization. The Chinese thus became the first nationality to be legally barred from the United States, despite the fact that the roughly123,000 Chinese immigrants arriving between 1871 and 1880 constituted only about 4.4 percent of the total number of immigrants during that time.[16] Although foreign-born Chinese were barred from citizenship, it was not clear if the Fourteenth Amendment conferred citizenship to U.S.-born Chinese children.[17] On March 28, 1898, the U.S. Supreme Court answered that question in the case of the *United States v. Wong Kim Ark*.[18]

Wong Kim Ark was born in 1873 in San Francisco, California. His parents were born in China.[19] They lived and had a business in San Francisco until 1890, when his parents returned to China. His parents were not diplomats and were never employed in an official capacity for the emperor of China, a fact that would become important to the case. Wong Kim Ark himself was a laborer. In 1890, when Wong was about 17 years old, he traveled to China. Upon returning to the United States, he was admitted as a native-born citizen with no problems. However, he traveled to China again in 1894, and on his return to the United States this time he was denied entry on the grounds that he was not a citizen of the United States. Wong Ark Kim claimed he was born in the United States and was therefore a U.S. citizen.

In deciding the case, the Court had to consider the meaning of the words "all persons born or naturalized in the United States, and subject to the jurisdiction thereof, are citizens of the United

States." The Court began with an interpretation of English common law, as the original framers of the Constitution would have understood it. The common law of England held that those born within the kingdom were natural-born subjects of the king. Even children born to foreign, or alien, parents who lived in the kingdom, either as settlers or sojourners, were also natural-born subjects. An exception was made for parents who were ambassadors, diplomats, or alien enemies. These categories of parents were not under the allegiance and jurisdiction of the king but were held to be under the jurisdiction of their own government, as were their children. (Diplomats and their families in the current world continue to hold a similar diplomatic immunity when it comes to the laws of the country where they are stationed.) As the Court put it, "'Natural-born British subject' means a British-subject who has become a British subject at the moment of his birth."

This relationship between birth and citizenship was in force in the American colonies and continued into the new United States. Justice Horace Gray cited Chancellor James Kent, who in the early 1800s wrote *Commentaries on American Law*: "Natives are all persons born within the jurisdiction and allegiance of the United States. This is the rule of the common law, *without any regard or reference to the political condition or allegiance of their parents*, with the exception of the children of ambassadors, who are in theory born within the allegiance of the foreign power they represent" (emphasis added).

So even as Wong Kim Ark's parents were unqualified for citizenship because of their race, their political status was irrelevant, according the Court. The important point, for the Court, was that Wong Kim Ark was born in the territory of the United States, placing him under the jurisdiction of the government and its laws, policies, and responsibilities. Justice Horace Gray emphasized this point with a quote from an article appearing in 1854 in the *American Law Register*: "The child of an alien, if born in the country, is as much a citizen as the natural born child of a citizen."

The Court also went to great lengths to make clear that the phrase "under the jurisdiction thereof" meant that the child, at the moment of birth, and the parents living in the United States, were subject to the laws and authority of the state and its government. As Justice Horace Gray noted, "It can hardly be denied that an alien is completely subject to the political jurisdiction of the country in which he resides." Residents of foreign birth, according to the Court, living in the United States and "mingling indiscriminately with its inhabitants for the purposes of business or pleasure" are never exempt from the jurisdiction and laws of the country. While in the country, they owe allegiance to the country and those laws. "Thus, Congress, when dealing with the question in that aspect, treated aliens residing in this country as 'under the jurisdiction of the United States.'" Because Wong Kim Ark's parents were subject to the jurisdiction of the United States, the Fourteenth Amendment guaranteed him birthright citizenship.

By deciding that Wong Kim Ark was a citizen by birth, as guaranteed by the Fourteenth Amendment, the Supreme Court made it clear that citizenship was a birthright not limited by race or parents' political status.[20] The Court's decision thus attempted to assure that children of stigmatized immigrant groups would not become a caste of internal minorities without citizenship, perhaps, for generations.[21] The Court also made it clear that while Congress has the power to regulate naturalization, the Fourteenth Amendment did not confer upon Congress the authority to restrict birthright citizenship.

In 1884, *Elk v. Wilkins* found an exception to birthright citizenship existed for Native Americans, which made clearer the issue of "jurisdiction thereof" and thus why the children of immigrants are citizens by birth. Native Americans were born within the borders of the United States, but they were viewed as living apart in tribes, considered "alien nations, distinct political communities" not under the jurisdiction of the United States and not subject to taxation. As independent and sovereign nations living on designated "Indian lands" and reservations, with their own police forces, courts, and governmental systems, they were not "under the jurisdiction thereof" of the United States any more than diplomatic representatives of foreign countries living in U.S. territory would be.[22] As the Court put it:

> The forgoing considerations and authorities irresistibly lead us to these conclusions: the Fourteenth Amendment affirms the ancient and fundamental rule of citizenship by birth within the territory, in the allegiance and under the protection of the country, including all children here born of resident aliens, with the exceptions or qualifications (as old as the rule itself) of children of foreign sovereigns or their ministers, or born on foreign public ships, or of enemies within and during a hostile occupation of part of our territory, and with the single additional exception of children of members of the Indian tribes owing direct allegiance to their several tribes.

As a consequence, Native Americans were not granted birthright citizenship under the Fourteenth Amendment until 1924. The children of immigrants born on U.S. soil were not exceptions to birthright citizenship because, unlike Native Americans, they were governed by the laws of the United States.

CHILDREN OF IMMIGRANTS AS PERPETUAL FOREIGNERS

Throughout the last decades of the nineteenth century, many questioned the ability of "new" immigrants' children to assimilate and there were continued attempts to amend the Fourteenth Amendment because of the alleged threat U.S.-born children of immigrants could pose. On May 15, 1880, an editorial in the *New York Times* compared European immigrants and their U.S.-born children's inability to assimilate to indigestion, stating that "A bad Irish-American boy is about as unwholesome a product as was ever reared in any body politic."[23] Similarly, the U.S.-born children of southern and eastern European immigrants were considered "too foreign." Francis A. Walker, superintendent of the U.S. Census of 1870 and 1889, made similar comments about the U.S.-born children of immigrants from Italy, Greece, Hungary, Russia, and other countries in southern and eastern Europe:

> Although born among us, our general instinctive feeling testifies that they are not wholly of us. So separate has been their social life, due alike to their clannishness and to our reserve; so strong have been the ties of race and blood and religion with them; so acute has been the jealousy of their spiritual teachers to our institutions—that we think of them, and speak of them, as foreigners.[24]

In 1920, Senator James D. Phelan, a Democrat from California, proposed a constitutional amendment to deny citizenship to "all Japanese born on American soil": only persons "whose parents are white, Africans, American Indians or their descendants and all persons naturalized in the United States and subject to the jurisdiction thereof would be eligible for citizenship." Phelan, like many others in California at the time, feared the Japanese would own all the state's farmland. He believed that "It is necessary, therefore, to deny citizenship to Japanese born on our soil and discourage their presence, thus preventing race conflicts and saving the white population from destruction."[25]

Because of Japanese immigrant involvement in farming, California made it difficult for them, as noncitizens, to own farmland. The Japanese, however, bought farmland in their U.S.-born children's names, which California's Alien Land Law made illegal. In 1922, the California Supreme Court struck down the California Alien Land Law and ruled that Japanese immigrants could serve as guardians for agricultural lands owned by their U.S.-born children. The Court reaffirmed that Japanese children were U.S. citizens by birth and could not be denied privileges enjoyed by other citizens because of their "race or color."[26]

The Court's ruling did not lessen the efforts to change the Fourteenth Amendment. In April 1931, as the nation experienced the Great Depression, the Women's Club Federation met in Fresno, California, to debate a resolution recommending that the California legislature adopt a law to ban citizenship to the children of immigrants born in the state. The arguments in its favor spoke of the "burdens imposed on California by alien invasion." As Mrs. Bradford Woodridge, a member of the state legislature put it:

> A curse is upon us here in California because of the Fourteenth Amendment. Hundreds of Japanese, Hindus, and Chinese are buying up our land. A wife who comes to join one of them and bears a baby two minutes after she lands, may have that child as a future citizen of the United States. And yet if that child is a Japanese he will owe allegiance to Japan for forty-six years and may be compelled by the law of the land of his parents to take arms in war against the United States.[27]

Concerns with an alleged Japanese American threat intensified after the United States entered World War II. Between 110,000 and 120,000 Japanese Americans were forcefully placed in internment camps during the war, many of them U.S.-citizens by birth. In April 1941, Jefferson D. Atwood, national vice-commander of the American Legion, speaking in Los Angeles, urged the group to support eliminating birthright citizenship for children of immigrants. Rather than allowing citizenship at birth, Atwood argued that "Our American citizenship must be guarded more closely than ever now, and it must be denied to the unworthy. I say to you that the child of the alien born in this country should become a citizen only after he becomes an adult and requests and qualifies for citizenship."[28] In September 1942, with the United States at war with Japan, the State Federation of Labor held their convention in Long Beach, California, and proposed that the citizenship of all Japanese born in the United States be revoked, and that they be prohibited from ever becoming citizens in the future. However, in December, the Los Angeles County grand jury objected to excluding "the entire Japanese race" from citizenship, including those born in the United States. "This would work a hardship on the 5,000 loyal Japanese now serving in the United States armed forces," the grand jury noted.[29]

LEGAL INCLUSION AND SOCIAL EXCLUSION

The U.S. Constitution's Fourteenth Amendment and Supreme Court cases have legally defined birthright citizenship to include the children of immigrants born on U.S. territory. However, legal definitions and court cases did not always protect the civil rights of the children of immigrants, as the internment of Japanese Americans attests. But the dark days of discrimination and fights over citizenship did not end with the war. Even though birthright citizenship defines both the citizen and the nation, new issues arose as immigration increased and as Latin Americans and Asians made up larger proportions of the nation's demographic profile.

While U.S.-born children have access to schools, this was not always the case with their undocumented siblings. The increasing presence of families with undocumented children led to a major court case in Texas to determine whether or not the state could bar undocumented children from state-funded public schools. The U.S. Supreme Court's ruling in the 1982 *Plyler v. Doe* case underscored the universal applicability of the Fourteenth Amendment. The Court ruled that all children, even undocumented children, had a right to education, and it was in the state's interest to ensure their education. The Court specifically took note of the issue of whether or not undocumented immigrants were under the jurisdiction of the state. As the Court noted:

> The Fourteenth Amendment to the Constitution is not confined to the protection of citizens only. It says: "Nor shall any state deprive any person of life, liberty, or property without due process of law; nor deny to any person within its jurisdiction equal protection of the laws."

These provisions are universal in their application, to all persons within the territorial jurisdiction, without regard to any differences of race, of color, or of nationality, and the protection of the laws is a pledge of the protection of the equal laws." (emphasis in original)

In other words, undocumented parents are under the jurisdiction thereof the United States, as are their U.S.-born children.[30]

In sum, for two hundred years the law has increasingly moved toward inclusionary citizenship. Once reserved for white males, today African Americans, Latinos, Asian Americans, and Native Americans are all guaranteed birthright citizenship. Claiming that the children of undocumented immigrants were not born "under the jurisdiction" of the United States is not new. The Supreme Court considered that argument during an earlier period of large-scale immigration and nativism and declared in no uncertain terms that children of immigrants, if born on U.S. territory, were indeed citizens.

Americans often pride themselves on their differences from the way the rest of the world does things, especially Great Britain and Europe. Allowing membership in the nation by birth is an excellent example of this American exceptionalism; the willingness to go our own way on citizenship distinguishes the United States. However, this does not mean that everyone agrees with the extension of birthright citizenship to anyone and everyone born in the United States. Who deserves to be citizens and the benefits they can expect as citizens is increasingly contested in the courts and in state and national legislative bodies.

Since 1965, the challenge to birthright citizenship has gained new strength with increased immigration, both legal and unauthorized. More immigration from non-European countries has meant increasing racial, cultural, and religious diversity. Periods of economic growth produce a demand for labor that at times has outpaced native fertility rates and an aging population, resulting in immigrant labor, both legal and unauthorized. A hardening

U.S.-Mexico border has meant more undocumented settlers raising families. Such changes set the stage for the emergence of the anchor baby in political discourse as well as political and legal contestations over birthright citizenship so evident in the previous chapter. But what of the costs inflicted on those who bear the burden of hardening immigration and deportation policies? Here we must include citizens so easily referred to as anchor babies, because they do not lead lives separate from immigrant family members.

Sensing an opportunity to take action rather than just talk about anchor babies, Texas in 2013 began denying birth certificates to U.S.-born children if their parents could not provide acceptable proof of identification.[1] In July 2015, Hiram Ramirez, a native of Mexico, went to the Texas Vital Statistics office in McAllen to get her daughter her birth certificate, just as she had done for her two older daughters. This time, however, she was told that the rules had changed and she would need to provide an acceptable form of identification: driver's license, military ID, passport or permanent residence card, or a Mexican electoral card.[2] These are often hard to get for undocumented immigrants living in Texas. Importantly, Texas would no longer accept the *matriculas consulares*, the identification cards issued by Mexican consulates, even though these cards are difficult to falsify, especially now that they are embedded with microchips. One city secretary in McAllen said they were just following state directives and that families have alternatives; they could bring a relative in with proper documentation to apply for the baby's birth certificate.[3] Lost in this explanation, or willingly ignored, is that the birth certificates are for U.S. citizens, not their parents.

Citizens living with families that include undocumented immigrants may be subject to policies that diminish their rights as citizens, or they may face verbal and physically aggressive behavior by individuals who challenge their right to belong in America. They also face the daily threat of deportation that would tear apart their families, often leaving them destitute. State policies that deny birth certificates to U.S.-born children not only affect the individuals so denied; they also underscore that the state can disregard the rights of these so-called anchor babies. Such policies also provide evidence of the power of anchor baby rhetoric to justify policies based on the belief that anchor babies are undeserving citizens.

The ostensible reason that the Texas Vital Statistics unit had been refusing to issue birth certificates in these cases was to prevent identity theft. At the time, Donald Trump was questioning the legitimacy of citizenship for anchor babies and promising he would deny their right to citizenship if he became president.[4] Also important was the context for Texas's new birth certificate rules, including opposition in Texas to President Obama's executive actions, Deferred Action for Childhood Arrivals (DACA) and Deferred Action for Parents of Americans and Lawful Permanent Residents (DAPA).[5] Beginning in June 2012, DACA allowed undocumented immigrants who were brought as children, before age 16, to the United States and who went to school there, or were honorably discharged from the U.S. military, to apply for a two-year renewable relief from deportation. They could also get a Social Security card and work. DACA was not a legalization program, offering only temporary protection from deportation. President Trump could rescind DACA, rendering DACA recipients deportable. DAPA would have provided temporary relief from deportation for undocumented parents of U.S. citizens and lawful permanent residents, thus reducing family separations (discussed in more detail below).

With hundreds of families unable to obtain birth certificates for their newborn children, lawyers for the Texas Civil Rights Project filed, on August 21, 2015, an emergency application for a preliminary injunction to stop the vital statistics offices in Texas from denying birth certificates, citing the irreparable harm inflicted by the policy.[6] The lawsuit was brought on behalf of 32 parents and 35 children denied birth certificates in the Rio Grande Valley. On October 16, 2015, Judge Robert L. Pitman denied the injunction, calling instead for a full hearing on the birth certificate issue.[7] In the meantime, Texas can continue to withhold birth certificates on the basis of a parent's inability to provide proper identification.

Although denying the injunction, the judge underscored the importance of the case and the role of birth certificates in establishing citizenship and its privileges. The defendants (Texas Department of State Health Services) argued that there were not sufficient facts to establish the need for a birth certificate to obtain the benefits and privileges of citizenship. The judge disagreed: "It simply begs credulity for Defendants to argue a birth certificate is not a vitally important document. The rights and privileges of citizenship inure to those who are citizens. The lack of a birth certificate, or other documentation establishing citizenship, presents a clear bar to access to those rights."[8] The judge emphasized this point in his conclusion:

> The Court has concluded the Plaintiffs have presented evidence showing that a lack of a birth certificate affects the fundamental rights of the citizen, Plaintiff children and the fundamental right of family integrity for both the Plaintiff children and parents. Insofar as a birth certificate is the primary means of documenting citizenship, it follows that a citizen's right to obtain it is as fundamental as the rights and privileges that flow from the status it documents.[9]

On July 22, 2016, Texas agreed in mediation to a settlement in the birth certificate case.[10] While not changing the policy requiring identification, nor accepting the Mexican consulate cards (*matriculas consulares*), Texas agreed to expand the types of documents it would accept from parents. Importantly, Texas would now accept Mexican voter identification cards issued by consulates in the

United States rather than cards issued only in Mexico. Central Americans could now get acceptable identification documents from their consulates in the United States as well. Jon Feere, legal analyst for the Washington-based Center for Immigration Studies, which advocates for restrictive immigration policies, commented: "This is yet another example of how our institutions are being asked to accommodate foreigners who think they are above the law."[11] However, Efrén Olivares, legal director of the Texas Civil Rights Project, South Texas office, and lead lawyer in the lawsuit, praised the settlement: "The bottom line is, there was a category of people who were being locked out of obtaining a birth certificate to which they are entitled constitutionally as citizens born in the United States just because of the immigration status of their parents."[12]

The controversy over birth certificates in Texas provides insights into what happens when the heated rhetoric over anchor babies turns into practice. Denying birth certificates to children if their parents are unable to provide acceptable proof of identification can have dire consequences and is an example of the violence the law can create in people's lives.[13] Affidavits filed as part of a lawsuit illustrate the problems families have encountered because of the lack of birth certificates for their children.[14] Estrella's husband took their son, born in Rio Grande City, Texas, to a very dangerous part of Mexico, where the drug war is ongoing. When a child was killed near the local school, she worried about her son and wanted him brought back to the United States. Without a birth certificate, she cannot get a passport for her son, which in turn makes it impossible for him to return safely to his own country of birth.

Nancy, a native of Mexico, had lived in Texas for seven years and had three children born in the United States. Although she had the birth papers provided by the hospital, she was denied birth certificates because she only had the Mexican *matricula* card and her husband's Mexican electoral card was expired. Nancy could not baptize her children without their birth certificates. Two of her children have mental health problems and faced cutoff of their Medicaid, which pays for their medicine, unless they brought in their birth certificates. One of her other children faced expulsion from school unless he brought in his birth certificate. The family faces removal from Section 8 housing unless they can bring in birth certificates to prove their children's citizenship. Nancy and her husband worry constantly about being apprehended and not being able to prove their children were born in the United States. "We also worry a lot about being approached by the police or the *migra* [immigration agents]. What would happen to our kids then? How can we establish they are truly our children?"

Juana had lived in Texas for 19 years, having come at the age of 14. She had three children born in Texas. When she went to get her young daughter's birth certificate, she provided the hospital's birth documents, her daughter's Social Security card, her own new Mexican *matricula* card with a microchip and valid until 2020, and her own Mexican passport that was also up-to-date. Her request for her daughter's birth certificate was denied because these forms of identification were no longer accepted. "They told me that I needed to bring in my [Mexican] election card. But I left Mexico when I was a minor and now I can't get it." Without her daughter's birth certificate, Juana has not been able to baptize her daughter, enroll her in the Head Start program, or enroll her into day care.

> Two months ago, when I tried to pass the immigration check point at Falfurrias [Texas], the officials did not want to let my daughter pass because she did not have her birth certificate. I felt very frustrated and humiliated because my daughter is a citizen of this country, and she has all the same rights as other citizens. After this incident, I worried a lot that the immigration agents could detain my daughter because she does not have documents that show she is an American citizen.

The application of the policy appears to be unevenly applied. Cynthia provided her Mexican electoral card and her husband provided a driver's license, as well as his Mexican *matricula* card, to the official in Cameron County, Texas, but they were denied their daughter's birth certificate. Cynthia's daughter was born with a strep infection, requiring immediate medical care and follow-up with specialists, including a neurologist. Cynthia's baby was enrolled in Medicaid, but Cynthia has been told that unless she provides a birth certificate her daughter would lose her Medicaid coverage. Like others, Cynthia and her husband worry about being apprehended and deported. "How can we prove that she is our daughter? If we are removed from the United States, how would she ever get back here to claim her citizenship?"

Maria, a resident of Texas for 14 years, was originally from Mexico. Twice immigration officials had stopped her, asking if the baby was hers and where the baby was born. Fortunately, Maria carried the birth papers issued by the hospital. They told her she needed the birth certificate if she is stopped in the future. Maria worries that she will be stopped and will not be able to prove she is her daughter's mother, and that they will take her away.

Quenia, originally from Mexico, had lived in Texas for more than ten years. She had a ten-year-old son who was born in Mission, Texas. Back then she had no problem getting his birth certificate. But about four years ago, her ex-husband returned to Mexico, taking her son's birth certificate and Social Security card with him. Quenia thought it would be easy to get a replacement birth certificate, but that was not the case.

> My mother and I and even my sister have gone to the birth certificate office in McAllen to try to replace [his] birth certificate. They turned me down. So my mother tried with her Mexican electoral card. They told her to get a *matricula*, but then turned that down as well. They also turned down my sister's Mexican electoral card, driver's license, and *matricula*. In 2015 I got the new *matricula* with the microchip in it but they turned this down. I have not been able to get a birth certificate for my new baby either. He was born in Edinburg, Texas in 2015.

Quenia has had trouble with schools and Medicaid because of the lack of birth certificates. She also worries about being detained and unable to prove that her children are U.S. citizens and that they are her children.

Many more stories could be told, but they would simply add weight to what is clear: the cumulative injurious effect of not having a birth certificate. These families do not experience one problem here and another there. Each family has experienced multiple problems, all of which place a great deal of stress on lives already strained by the parents' immigration status. Now they have to worry about the effects of limited access to medical care and education on their children's development. They also fear children will be taken from the family because they cannot prove they are their children. Deportation is also a great fear because they do not know how their U.S.-citizen children would be able to return to the United States, or be able to get their birth certificates, from the other side of the border.

In short, denying birth certificates is tantamount to denying these children the privileges, protections, and rights of citizenship guaranteed by the Fourteenth Amendment as a birthright. What is accomplished by imposing such a burden on these U.S.-born children and their families, especially given that not providing birth certificates raises constitutional issues? One answer might be that Texas is sending the message that the state can treat these children differently from other citizens. By creating obstacles to acquiring birth certificates, Texas is also sending the message to the children of immigrants that they are not real citizens, that they are unwanted, and that they do not belong despite their birthright. It is a message applauded by those who favor the anchor baby rhetoric and view denying birthright citizenship as a means to reducing immigration.

However, invoking anchor babies, birth certificates, and citizenship also sends a message that extends beyond immigrants and their children. It suggests to all Mexican Americans, and even all Latinos, that even if you are born in this county you are still suspect citizens. That is also the anchor baby metaphor's message, one that is reaffirmed every time a citizen is asked, "Are you an anchor baby?" for no apparent reason. Or when state or school administrators raise questions about a citizen child's parents' residency or identification; or when a waiter asks for proof of U.S. legal residency before serving a customer; or when someone shouts, "Go back where you came from," even though where you came from is the United States.[15] The anchor baby can become a mark of Cain extending beyond first-generation Americans, as one sixth-generation citizen found out when he woke to find his van spray-painted with the word "illegal" across it.[16]

MIXED-STATUS FAMILIES

One of the problems with all the talk about "anchor babies" and "illegal immigrants" is how much these terms are used to conflate the complexity of people's lives into simple types. For example, "illegal alien families," or even "immigrant families," are relatively rare. More often, families with immigrants are "mixed" families. They consist of a mix of many possible immigration or citizenship statuses.[17] Some are U.S. citizens, some might be unauthorized to reside in the United States, while others might be legal permanent residents or in the process of becoming a legal permanent resident.

The growth of mixed families was an unintended consequence of "get tough" immigration laws. One of the key provisions of the 1986 Immigration Reform and Control Act was increased funding for border surveillance leading to an increased militarization of the border.[18] As a result, the U.S.-Mexico border became more difficult and dangerous to cross clandestinely by land.[19] Once in the United States, undocumented migrants now had greater incentive to stay rather than return home and risk another border crossing back into the United States.[20] This fear of recrossing the border is especially true for women and children. Increased border enforcement made frequent return migration after a few months of work more difficult, leading to migrants staying in the United

States longer and forming families, thus increasing the settled undocumented population.[21]

As undocumented migrants establish families, they have children born in the United States. Evidence of this trend is provided by the increase in annual U.S. births to unauthorized immigrants since 1980 (see Figure 3). It should be noted, however, that as with all questions about numbers related to a population that lives in the shadows of the law, we must rely on estimates. Some estimates are better than others. Some estimates from advocates for immigration restrictions have gone as high as 574,000 to 726,000 children born annually to undocumented mothers living in the Untied States.[22] According to the Pew Research Center, however, the number of children born in the United States to undocumented immigrants has declined since the peak of 370,000 in 2007, the year before the Great Recession. In 2008, immigration began to decline and so did the number of children to undocumented immigrants.[23] In 2014, about 275,000 babies were born to undocumented parents. There were between 4.7 and 6.6 million U.S.-born children living with at least one undocumented parent in 2014.[24]

As the number of births to undocumented immigrants increased, its share of all births in the United States also increased. In 1980, the Pew Research Center found that U.S.-born children born to undocumented immigrants accounted for only 1 percent of all births. Their share of all births peaked in 2005–7, right before the Great Recession, when they accounted for 9 percent of all births. Since then, births to undocumented parents have declined as undocumented immigration declined. In 2014, births to undocumented immigrants accounted for 7 percent of all births.

In my book *Shadowed Lives*, I coined the term "binational families" to capture the complexity of legal statuses and nationalities.[25] The problem is not with these families but with the perceived threat they pose, especially when all family members are characterized as "illegal immigrants" regardless of their status.

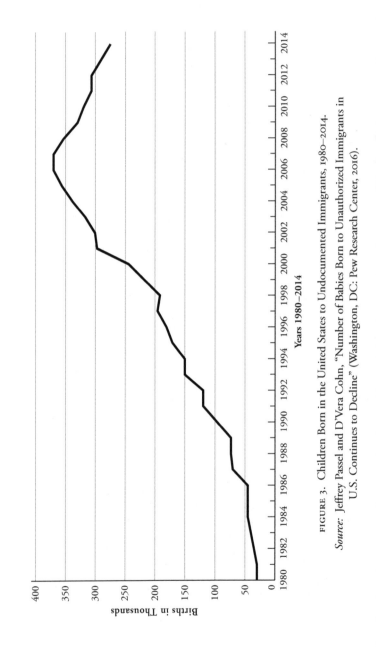

FIGURE 3. Children Born in the United States to Undocumented Immigrants, 1980–2014.

Source: Jeffrey Passel and D'Vera Cohn, "Number of Babies Born to Unauthorized Immigrants in U.S. Continues to Decline" (Washington, DC: Pew Research Center, 2016).

I can still sense the fear and confusion young Carolina (pseud-onym) felt when she spoke of what might happen to her family after her mother had been detained by the immigration authorities while riding a bus in San Diego. Carolina was 13 at the time, and although born in Mexico she was brought to the United States as a baby. She worried about being deported to Mexico, where she had little experience, and about her little brother, age 11, who was born in the United States.

> I was worried that we were going to be sent back to Mexico, that we had to go back and live like those people, without any homes. They have to sleep in the streets, sell anything, like gum. There was going to be no food. Maybe I couldn't go to school because my parents needed money. . . . We were going to lose everything we had here. . . . I was afraid that maybe my brother had to stay here, and we had to go, because he's an American citizen. And maybe the government would send him to some kind of shelter for kids that don't have homes or anything. Maybe he was going to miss his parents and me.[26]

Carolina's characterizations of life in Mexico reflected child-hood understandings and fears rather than actual life in Mexico. But they capture her fear of deportation and despair of a pending rupture to her life and family. Sadly, stories such as Carolina's continue today. A young Filipina woman recently wrote of her many years living as an undocumented immigrant. She was brought to the United States by her mother when she was five years old. She became a citizen at age 28, having lived until then in fear of being found and deported. "My biggest fear was that my little sister, a citizen, would grow up alone—that one day she would wake up alone because deportation agents had taken us in the middle of the night. I had heard stories of it happening to others around me. If a classmate stopped coming to school, rumors would swirl around. La migra. We could always be next."[27]

U.S.-born children of immigrants are raised in families where the immigrant experience is fresh and an everyday part of their lives. However, they are not immigrants but American citizens. Terms that erase this important distinction can lead to citizens being thought of as immigrants, anchor babies, or undeserving, even suspect citizens who are part of their immigrant family's plot to gain legal status. Or they could be part of a broader conspiracy by Mexico to take over the United States. Such characterizations easily transform into challenges to the Fourteenth Amendment and birthright citizenship for these children. It can also lead to other attempts to punish these families.

U.S.-born children can be caught up in mass deportations, as occurred during the Great Depression when hundreds of thousands of Mexican families, including U.S.-born children, were rounded up and repatriated to Mexico.[28] In Paul Espinosa's docudrama *The Lemon Grove Incident*, one man spoke about the distress he experienced when his family was deported. Although he was born in Mexico, he had five brothers and sisters who were born in the United States and were therefore citizens. The emotional toll was still visible over 50 years later when, during the filming of the docudrama, he talked about what had happened:

> They took advantage [of our family] because we were supported by the government, because my father had died. According to them [the government]. It was for that reason we were sent back. And I had five brothers and sisters born here. You spend half of your life here in the States, and they throw you back to a country you have not lived in very much. Then you don't know which country you have to belong to first.[29]

Being discarded from the country where you grew up, or having family members torn away, leaves an emotional scar that can last a lifetime.[30] Unfortunately, such experiences have become ever more common. It must be noted that deportations do not affect all nationalities equally. Mexicans accounted for about 53 percent of the undocumented population in 2010, but about 73 percent of the deportations. Immigrants from Asian and European countries accounted for about 15 percent of the unauthorized at that time, but only about 3 percent of deportations.[31]

I once submitted a sworn affidavit against a Department of Health and Urban Development proposal to remove "illegal alien families" from federally subsidized public housing. The problem, I wrote, was that more often than not denying a whole family public housing (or any social service) on the basis of one member's immigration status would mean denying U.S. citizens housing to which they have as much right as any other citizen.

While pernicious, such policies pale in comparison to the trauma experienced when families are divided by deportation.[32] The alleged benefits of having an anchor baby can evaporate in a second with deportation. Having a citizen child does not protect undocumented family members from being apprehended and returned to their country of origin.

DEPORTATION AS PUBLIC POLICY

Over the last 40 years, deportations have risen steadily. It is difficult to compare deportation statistics over time due to changing definitions, but Figure 4 displays a relatively good comparison of removals (typically by court order, such as deportation orders), and does not include "returns," which used to be called "voluntary departures" by apprehended border-crossers.

For much of the 20th century, deportations (again, as distinct from the immediate return of apprehended border-crossers) were relatively few, except during the Great Depression in the 1930s and a couple of years in the 1950s during Operation Wetback, in which Mexican workers were rounded up and deported. From 1970 until the mid-1980s, the number of deportations or removals averaged about 17,000 a year. The Immigration Reform and Control Act of 1986 increased immigration and border enforcement, and deportations began to rise slowly.[33] Removals surged dramatically during Bill Clinton's presidency, 1993–2001. The North Atlantic Free

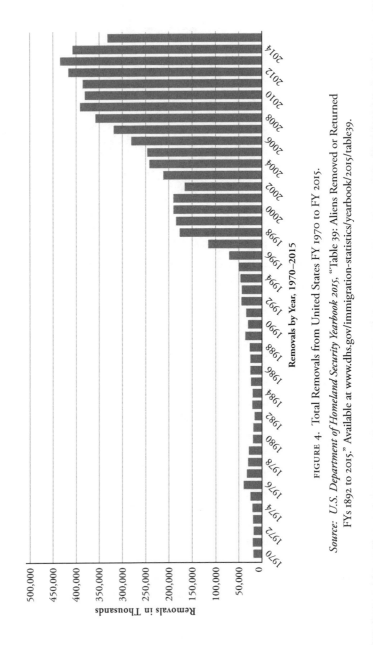

FIGURE 4. Total Removals from United States FY 1970 to FY 2015.

Source: U.S. Department of Homeland Security Yearbook 2015, "Table 39: Aliens Removed or Returned FYs 1892 to 2015." Available at www.dhs.gov/immigration-statistics/yearbook/2015/table39.

Trade Agreement (NAFTA) took effect in 1994, with an increase in displaced Mexican rural farmers moving north.[34] In 1996, President Clinton signed into law the Illegal Immigration Reform and Immigrant Responsibility Act. The 1996 immigration law contributed to the rising number of removals by making it easier to deport all immigrants, legal and undocumented, for crimes that previously were minor crimes, typically misdemeanors, which would not have resulted in deportation.

Removals continued to rise during George W. Bush's presidency, 2001–9, as calls for stricter immigration enforcement rose after 9/11. Deportations reached 359,795 in 2008, the last full year of Bush's administration. As Figure 4 indicates, deportations reached new heights during the Obama administration, beginning in 2009, hitting a peak of 435,498 removals in 2013. The notable rise in deportations led critics to refer to President Obama as the "Deporter-in-Chief."[35]

The number of deportations began to drop in 2014. However, since 1996 thousands of families with U.S. citizens have been split apart as one or more members, typically parents but sometimes spouses and siblings, were apprehended and removed from the country. An average of 90,000 parents of U.S.-citizen children were deported in 2011 and 2012, and about 72,000 in 2013.[36] Apart from these removal statistics are those migrants caught entering at the border who are then returned relatively quickly. According to Human Rights Watch, about 60 percent of parents of U.S.-born children detained at the border are summarily returned in ways that do not allow them the opportunity to make claims in front of a judge about their ties to family in the United States.[37]

Shortly after taking office, on January 25, 2017, President Trump issued Executive Order No. 13768: Enhancing Public Safety in the Interior of the United States.[38] Trump's order expanded deportable offenses to include virtually anyone in the country without authorization, in order to meet his campaign promise of deporting 11 million undocumented immigrants.[39] Since then, it seems as if every day brings new headlines of detentions, including DACA students and a father detained after dropping off his children at school, and of ICE officers coming to people's homes claiming to be local police, and a general fear among law-abiding undocumented immigrants who are now the target of immigration authorities.[40]

Statistics indicate just how prevalent the problem of living with deportation is for undocumented immigrants and their families. Removing undocumented members of mixed-status families, typically the breadwinner, could reduce household income from $41,300 to $22,000, which would reduce these families with U.S.-born children to poverty.[41] But we must not stop at elucidating this significant statistical pattern of expulsion. We also need to explore the subjective experiences of families, especially those with U.S. citizens, torn apart by deportation.[42] Birthright citizenship does not protect these children from having family deported, nor shield them from feelings of being abject, that is, of being society's outcasts, whose families are easily thrown away.[43] Sarah Willen coined the term "abjectivity" to highlight the subjective understanding of living an abject life that can penetrate a person's very being.[44] Stories of living in the aftermath of losing family to deportation are filled with a range of deeply felt emotions, from angst and despair to courage and hope. Such stories often find their way into the media, including the *Los Angeles Times* and the *New York Times*, in the attempt to portray the human side of immigration policies.

DEPORTATION AS FAMILY TRAUMA

With thousands of families affected by deportation, it would take up too much space to give each and every deserving story its due. We can, however, provide examples that illustrate the significant moments in a family's experience with deportation.[45] These moments include the fear and impact of deportation, apprehension, and incarceration, the emotional, financial, and educational toll deportation leaves in its wake, and decisions about keeping family together or splitting the family across national borders.

Fear of apprehension, detention, and deportation has risen along with the increased deportation rates. By 2001, tens of thousands of immigrants had been deported, and the Immigration and Naturalization Service housed many others in federal prisons or in one of the 225 remote jails spread around the country, where they could languish for years.[46] Parents fear deportation because of the unknown fate of their children. Some fear that their children, even U.S. citizens, will be put up for adoption.[47] Fear of losing their children if deported is a real fear as many children are placed in foster homes.[48] More often, children of deported immigrants are taken care of by a remaining parent or extended family member, or even a friend.

Often deportation creates single-parent families, but sometimes the one single parent or both parents can be picked up and removed. In either case, families can lose everything, experiencing a quick decline into poverty.[49] Antoni Runierc, who came from Poland in 1980, was convicted for driving a car with stolen plates, which he claimed were on a car belonging to one of the customers of his auto body shop in Amherst, Massachusetts. The bank foreclosed on his house and he could not afford to pay for legal representation. Incarcerated and awaiting deportation in 2001, he talked about the impact on his U.S.-born children: "Everything my wife and I built for ourselves in this country has been taken away from us. We are ruined. My oldest daughter is being treated for depression. My two younger children, at this point, do not even know their father."[50]

Families are often thrown into chaos when apprehensions suddenly occur. Family members may not know the fate of those apprehended, or how to contact children. In the fall of 2004, Adnan Thakur and his two-year-old sister, both U.S. citizens, were asleep when immigration agents came to their house in Jamaica, Queens, and took their mother away in handcuffs. She was an undocumented immigrant from Bangladesh who worked as a cashier in a hardware store, and her husband was a legal immigrant who drove a cab. Theirs was a binational, or mixed, family. The family decided to send the children to Bangladesh with their mother. Adnan and his sister waited on the plane for their mother, but the immigration agents had not acquired the proper documents and returned her to detention, leaving the children on the plane with a colleague of their father. By the time their mother was able to join them in Bangladesh, the children had been living for ten days with strangers. In a call to his father, Adnan said, "I want to go home to America." But that was not possible.[51]

For citizen and noncitizen children, just thinking about deportation's impact on the family can magnify the possible pathos and trauma that await them. This fear of being deportable can be just as devastating as deportation itself, leading to self-monitoring behavior such as avoiding medical appointments, not seeking help from police, or staying at home and avoiding "dangerous" public spaces, even going to the grocery store.[52] Students have even begun to avoid student loans to further their education for fear that their parents' information will be provided to immigration authorities.[53] Tragically, derailing education for their children is one of the greatest fears of immigrant parents. Benjamin Carbreras, a waiter, came from Mexico in the 1980s at about the same time that his wife, a teaching assistant, came from Guatemala. They have two U.S.-born daughters and found themselves facing possible deportation in 2006. Their oldest daughter is academically gifted and Benjamin believed her studies would be "savagely and permanently interrupted" if he and his wife were deported. As he said: "It's not right for us to be split up. It would destroy the whole family. We are not the only ones who would suffer. Our daughters would too." His daughter, who wants to attend college, acknowledged that despite her academic prowess, if her parents were deported her plans might be ruined.[54]

Fear of deportation leads to a sense of despair and the inability to plan for the future because of a possible unplanned encounter with immigration agents. Maria Flores, an undocumented immigrant from Mexico living in Los Angeles, has five children, the youngest a U.S. citizen. She dreads the possibility that her family will someday be split apart because of Congress's inability to agree on a comprehensive immigration bill. "We are planning a future for our children, but [politicians] are planning another future. They are deciding our lives."[55]

Children, regardless of citizenship status, can fear having their lives disrupted because they have to assume adult responsibilities for younger siblings should parents be deported. Marvin was 17 years old in 2006. He and his four younger siblings, all born in the United States, lived with their mother, who came from Mexico without authorization two decades earlier, and works two jobs to help support the family. Her partner also works and contributes to the family's upkeep. Marvin worries constantly about what would happen if his mother and stepfather were deported. "I'll work, but I can't support everyone."[56]

Adult citizens also experience the emotional trauma of deportation, often that of a spouse.[57] For example, in 2009, U.S. Army specialist Jack Barrios, 26, was suffering posttraumatic stress after his service in Iraq. Adding to his problems was that his wife, Frances, age 23, who was brought from Guatemala to the United States at age 6, was undergoing deportation proceedings, a problem faced by many U.S. soldiers whose spouses were foreign born. "She's my everything. Without her, I can't function. It would be like taking away a part of my soul." Their two U.S.-born children will remain with their father in the United States. But his wife worries: "I'm with them all day. I cook. I clean. It will be too much for Jack. It's hard enough for him already." Jack acknowledged that his wife broke the law by entering the country without authorization, but he argues that she was just a young child. "I just want my girl to stay here and be part of this country. Why should we have to break up our family? We just want to have the American Dream, just like everyone else."[58]

With little legal recourse, some children look for divine intervention in the face of their parents' deportation. In 2014, ten-year-old Jersey Vargas made a pilgrimage to Rome to meet the Pope and express the pain she and other children experience when their parents are taken from them and deported. Her father, born in Mexico, was caught driving without a license in Indiana, where he was working on a construction job, and was now under deportation proceedings. Before she left, she met with the Los Angeles archbishop Jose H. Gomez, himself a naturalized citizen. As Jersey said: "I came here so everyone could hear me and not ignore me, because I want them to feel the pain and how I'm feeling very sad because now I don't have my dad with me. And when I see other girls with their parents, I wish I were them." When asked what she would tell the Pope, Jersey said, "I'm going to introduce myself and where I'm from, and say I'm representing millions of children who today are in my situation . . . and I think it's unfair that people are separating families because right now is a time when kids really need their parents."[59]

A HOBSON'S CHOICE

Facing deportation, families with U.S.-born children have limited options. With little legal remedy, parents can take their children with them, a de facto deportation of citizen children.[60] Or citizen children can join their parents as they go further underground in the United States to escape deportation. They can also split their family across national borders. In other words, families face a number of equally bad and painful choices. Mr. Mancia and his wife Maria left Honduras in 2005 because of the high level of violence. Maria's sister was gunned down while riding a bus. Mr. Mancia and his wife were picked up in a raid on the leather goods factory where they worked in New Bedford, Massachusetts. Maria was kept in detention, while Mr. Mancia was released to take care of their two sons, including Jeffery, a U.S. citizen. Maria was deported quickly, even though she did not have a criminal record. Mr. Mancia had to decide to either take his sons with him to Honduras or leave them with friends in the United States, where he believed they could get a good education. "We walked over dead bodies in Honduras. The children see that and they don't grow up well. . . . My son is an American. He needs to be educated in American schools, to speak English. He needs this country."[61]

Some parents decide to leave their children in the United States, often in the care of a relative, but the children still carry a heavy emotional burden and responsibility for family care. Leslie, 16, her sister, Adilene, 8, and their brother Marcos, 13, all U.S. citizens, found themselves in that situation in 2007, when immigration agents came to their house, apprehended their parents, and deported them to Mexico. Their mother, speaking from Tijuana, explained their decision: "Being separated is very difficult, but why am I going to deprive them of their right to live there? There is no future here [in Mexico]. It's a very rough life here. I don't want that for my kids." And even though an aunt lives with the children, Leslie has adult responsibilities, feeding her siblings and making sure they get to school. "It's like I am a parent now. I have two children I am in charge of. They are dependent on me."[62] The children do not sleep in their own rooms but crowd into their parents' room. A knock on the door makes Adilene jump in fear, and she cries at night, looking at her parents' photograph. Adilene said: "Now that my parents are not here, I don't want to live in this house. I don't want to even go to school. I don't want to eat. I don't want to do anything." Leslie's grades suffered; once getting A's and B's, she now gets C's and D's.[63]

Sometimes just the fear of deportation can cause families to split apart. Originally from Mexico, Benigno and Gabriela had lived in the United States ten years and four years, respectively, as undocumented immigrants. On September 15, 2004, they had sextuplets at the UC San Diego Medical Center, the result of hormone treatment. They made a point of not accepting government assistance with the children, nor seeking media attention and the assistance that often accompanies such multiple births. They worked, paid taxes, and supported their children. One day, uniformed officers came and searched their apartment looking for the previous dweller, an undocumented immigrant. Gabriela was so fear stricken by the experience that she decided to return to Mexico, taking the six kids with her, leaving Benigno to work and send money. The children, age nine, would ask their mother why everyone calls them "gringos," and why they could not go see their father in California and sleep in their own beds. She would tell them: "Because I was born here. If I try to cross into the U.S., the police will take me to jail." As U.S. citizens, the children could return someday.[64]

Split families leave children perplexed about how to explain absent family, not wanting people to think that their deported parents are "bad people." Emma Sanchez Paulson was still breast-feeding her two-month-old son, and had two other sons age five and three, when she was deported in 2006. Emma was married to a U.S. citizen and military veteran, but when she went to the U.S. consulate in Ciudad Juarez for an appointment to adjust her status, the immigration official denied her entry and banned her from the United States for ten years. For the past nine years, her sons, U.S. citizens, and husband visited her in Tijuana every two weeks. At first, her sons were going to live with her in Tijuana, but she and her husband found the schools and standard of living less than that of the United States. Her sons are tired of the separation. Emma's 12-year-old son told her: "It makes me really angry when they [schoolmates] ask me where my mom is. I don't want to tell them. What do I tell them? How do I explain to them that you are a deported mother? They are going to think you are a bad person, and you are not a bad person."

When parents are deported, U.S.-citizen children are also forced to choose to stay in their own native country or leave with their parents to a country they do not know personally. This is precisely the decision described so compellingly by Dianne Guerrero, the actor, in her book *In the Country We Love.*

Dianne Guerrero's parents were from Colombia, and her family life changed dramatically when her parents were deported. "One moment—that's all it takes for your entire world to split apart. For me, that moment came when I was fourteen. I returned home from school to discover that my hardworking immigrant parents had been taken away. In one irreversible instant—in the space of a single breath—life as I'd known it was forever altered."[65] Dianne chose to stay in the United States because she believed that her dreams could only come true there rather than in Colombia, a country she had never visited. But the decision was not easy. It was as if her parents had died. "The summer I lost my parents it was the strangest kind of heartache. No friends gathered to grieve over the departed. No flowers were sent. No memorial service was planned. And yet the two people I'd cherished most were gone. Not gone from the world itself, but gone from me. We'd find a way to move forward, to carry on. Just not with the promise of one another's presence."[66]

Whatever possible benefit Dianne may have gotten by being an "anchor baby" was lost the day her parents were deported. Dianne and thousands of other so-called anchor babies have had family members deported, an experience that leaves in its wake families that are emotionally scarred and financially destitute.[67] Citizen children in these families experience the convergence of immigration law and criminal law, which creates intense moments of family trauma that can have years of lingering effects on their emotional well-being and social integration.[68]

DEFERRED ACTION FOR PARENTS OF AMERICANS (DAPA)

The term "anchor baby" signifies many things, but rarely does it capture the reality that these so-called anchor babies are citizens whose families can be torn apart by deportation of parents or siblings. Facing criticism for the high deportation rate and the subsequent splitting apart of families during most of his presidency, President Obama took executive action in an attempt to provide a measure of relief to undocumented parents of U.S. citizens. In November 2014, President Obama announced DAPA, Deferred Action for Parents of Americans and Lawful Permanent Residents. DAPA would have allowed some undocumented immigrants to stay in the United States without fear of deportation and work, for three years. To qualify, the applicant needed to have lived in the United States continuously since January 1, 2010, have no lawful status on November 20, 2014, have a child of any age or marital status who is a U.S. citizen or legal permanent resident, and have not been convicted of a felony or significant misdemeanor, or more than three misdemeanors, nor pose a threat to national security, nor be an enforcement priority for removal.[69] DAPA would, in essence, have provided temporary relief from many of the fears of deportation plaguing mixed families.[70]

DAPA added to the anchor baby controversy by creating the impression that undocumented immigrants with citizen children were to be given special treatment. However, DAPA became moot on February 16, 2015, when a federal district judge in Texas stopped the government from moving forward with the DAPA program. The court considered the president's power to issue an executive action such as DAPA rather than having Congress legislate immigration policy. The case went before the U.S. Supreme Court, which had been reduced to eight justices after the death of Justice Antonin Scalia. On June 23, 2016, the Court deadlocked with a four-to-four decision, effectively upholding the district court's ruling and stopping DAPA from being implemented.[71]

President Trump removed the possibility that DAPA could return to the Supreme Court in the future when he rescinded the DAPA program on June 15, 2017. As one headline put it: "Trump Rescinds Obama-Era Policy Protecting Parents of 'Anchor Babies.'" The other possible remedy would be that Congress pass comprehensive immigration reform, which would provide a path to citizenship for the undocumented members of these families. Although having come close in recent years, the U.S. Congress has been unable to reach a compromise on immigration reform. Immigrant families I have spoken with had moments of great hope when President Obama announced DAPA, and then as Congress appeared to move toward immigration reform, only to be deeply disappointed time and again, leaving them with a profound sense of despair. Consequently, there is no relief from deportation for families with U.S.-citizen children, nor is there likely to be in the near future.

Anchor babies may be accused of gaming the system and providing benefits to their parents in unfair ways, but if these examples can serve as a guide, their lives are anything but worry free. They live under the constant threat of forced family separation through deportation. Their citizenship is diminished and their sense of belonging shaken by the anchor baby rhetoric. They are subject to the whims of politicians who instigate policies that treat them as nonresidents or deny them birth certificates as punishment for their parents' unauthorized status. Although the courts may mitigate such policies, the message is sent and received: anchor babies are second-class citizens. Of course, "anchor babies" only exist in the minds of those who use this insulting and dehumanizing term. In reality, they are U.S. citizens and will continue to be citizens despite the anchor baby rhetoric's attempt to marginalize them and construct them as a threat to "legitimate" citizens.

EPILOGUE

Throughout American history the children of immigrants have lived liminal lives, betwixt and between their immigrant parents and the nation into which they were born. Feared as a threat to the nation at one time and then later recognized as the very identity of the nation can be unsettling for U.S.-born children of immigrants. However, one could argue that their history in America has been one of increasing inclusion, often through struggle. Fear of change, blaming, and scapegoating the children of immigrants, calling them anchor babies, hopefully will not change the trajectory of that history.

The Fourteenth Amendment to the U.S. Constitution declared citizenship by birth a fundamental right for all babies born on U.S. territory. Later, the U.S. Supreme Court made clear in the Wong Kim Ark case that the children of immigrants are citizens if born in the United States and under the jurisdiction thereof. Importantly, the Wong Kim Ark case affirmed birthright citizenship even in cases where immigrant parents were stigmatized by the larger society and declared ineligible for citizenship. Despite constitutional affirmations of birthright citizenship, the nation has engaged in often-heated political debates over the belonging and inclusion of immigrants and their children. The war of words and images has been intimately linked to restrictive immigration policies, nativist movements, immigration reform, and amnesties for unauthorized immigrants.[1] Shamefully, citizen children of immigrants have been caught up in anxieties over national security and seen their constitutional rights suspended.[2] The repatriation of U.S. citizens of Mexican descent during the 1930s Depression and the internment of Japanese Americans during World War II were infamous examples of suspended civil liberties, states of exception, during national emergencies.

It is difficult to assess the toll on one's psyche of being the subject of vitriolic anchor baby commentary. Imagine the emotional burden of continually being the target of mean-spirited bills in Congress to remove your birthright citizenship, which would leave you a person without a nation. Such inflammatory rhetoric may serve political ends, but it can cause a lot of collateral damage in its wake. So-called anchor babies must bear the pain of being called out as the Other in media and public discourse, and even by the president of the United States. They are made to feel as if they do not belong to the nation of which they feel so profoundly a part.

We have been told since childhood that "sticks and stones will break my bones, but words will never hurt me." But hurtful public discourse can cut to the bone and have lasting effects.[3] In a study I am conducting with colleagues at my university, we asked participants to read some quotes and view some images that capture positive and negative aspects of public discourse on immigration.[4] After viewing the negative portrayals of immigrants and "anchor babies," this young Mexican American woman said:

> Anger, rage, frustration, impotence are just some of the words that come to mind, but I have so much to say that I am not able to properly articulate what I am trying to say—much less express myself in a healthy manner. These types of aggressions are not new to me, so I know what it's like to have these words and images being shouted at you, and making you feel out of place, ashamed and inferior, even though you were born in the U.S.

As her comments suggest, processes of inclusion can be derailed for the children of immigrants when their lives are filled with grief and despair because their families are not fully free from the fear of deportation, or because they feel themselves the target of stigmatizing discourses, even if they are U.S. citizens.

The politics of citizenship sometimes are not pretty. They are often mean spirited, unconcerned with subtlety or the damage they can cause. Their goals are to undermine the belonging and legitimacy of the targets of such politics. Anchor babies are such targets. The problem is that once the Pandora's box of citizenship has been opened, there can be many targets. Think of the years President Obama had to endure questions about his birth certificate, with many "birther" conspiracy theorists claiming he was really born in Kenya, and of course that he was also a Muslim.[5] By raising the birth certificate issue, birthers were actually arguing that Obama was not a natural-born citizen and thus ineligible to be president of the United States, an argument reflecting deep-seated anxieties held by some over an African American being president.[6]

Republicans even questioned whether their own presidential candidates in 2016—John McCain, Ted Cruz, Marco Rubio, and Donald Trump—were natural-born citizens. John McCain was born in Panama, in the American-controlled Canal Zone, to parents who were U.S.-born citizens, which raised questions about his being a natural-born citizen.[7] Donald Trump raised questions about Ted Cruz's eligibility to be president given that he was born in Canada to a U.S.-citizen mother and Cuban immigrant father.[8] Trump also claimed Marco Rubio was not a natural-born citizen because even though he was born in Florida his parent were Cuban immigrants. Ted Cruz countered that the birther theory that Trump relies upon says that a person must have two parents born on U.S. soil to be a natural-born citizen. Cruz stated that if that were actually the case, which he did not agree with, "I would be disqualified [from being president], Marco Rubio would be,

Bobby Jindal would be disqualified. And Donald Trump would be disqualified."[9] Cruz included Trump because Trump's mother was born in Scotland. The old adage, "What goes around, comes around," seems to be at work here.

So-called anchor babies are not the only ones living in mixed families. Many of the Republican candidates for president in 2016 mentioned above lived in families consisting of citizens, immigrants, and refugees. Perhaps living in families with a mix of citizens and immigrants, races and ethnicities, religious beliefs, sexual orientation, or any combination of what constitutes the American mosaic defines what it means to be American.

Perhaps the most infamous case of questioning the belonging of a U.S. citizen because of his ethnic heritage occurred when Donald Trump denigrated Judge Gonzalo Curiel's integrity. The controversy began on May 27, 2016, at a rally in San Diego, California. For almost 11 minutes, Trump railed against U.S. district judge Curiel, who was presiding over civil fraud lawsuits brought against Trump and Trump University by former students. In Donald Trump's own words:

> So I end up in a lawsuit and it ends up in San Diego. And it's a disgrace how the federal court is acting. . . . The case should have been dismissed on summary judgment, everybody says it, but I have a judge that is a hater of Donald Trump. A hater. He's a hater. His name is Gonzalo Curiel. . . . We're in front of a very hostile judge. The judge was appointed by Barack Obama. Federal judge. Frankly he should recuse himself because he's given us ruling after ruling, negative, negative, negative. . . . The judge, who happens to be we believe Mexican, which is great, I think that's fine. . . . I think Judge Curiel should be ashamed of himself. I think it is a disgrace that he is doing this [not dismissing the case]. . . . They ought to look into Judge Curiel because what Judge Curiel is doing is a total disgrace.[10]

Although Trump called Judge Curiel a Mexican, he was actually born in Indiana. His parents, however, were from Mexico. A few days later, on June 3, in an interview with the *Wall Street Journal*, Trump attempted to clarify his remarks about Judge Curiel but only dug himself deeper into controversy. When it became clear that Curiel is American and not Mexican, Trump pointed to his Mexican heritage as presenting an "absolute conflict" to his ability to treat Trump fairly and without bias because of Trump's stance against illegal immigration and pledge to build a "huge" wall between Mexico and the United States. "I'm building a wall. It's an inherent conflict of interest."[11] The unprecedented act of a presidential candidate attacking a judge's ethnicity led to bipartisan criticism. Paul Ryan, the nation's highest-ranking Republican, commented: "Claiming a person can't do their job because of their race is sort of like the textbook definition of a racist comment. I think that should be absolutely disavowed. It's absolutely unacceptable."[12]

The important point here is that Judge Curiel is the U.S.-born son of Mexican immigrants, which puts him into the anchor baby category so reviled by Donald Trump and many others in favor of restricting immigration. While other judges might also disagree with Trump's immigration views and border wall plans, their views are not said to be innate to their nationality, ethnic heritage, or race. In Judge Curiel's case it is merely his ethnic heritage that raises a warning flag because his actual views on Trump's proposed policies are unknown. It is enough to call him a "Mexican" to assume what he believes and to underscore that because of his difference he cannot be trusted to be impartial. Raising Judge Curiel's heritage, like the anchor baby metaphor, sends the message that U.S.-born Mexican Americans are not like other citizens; their belonging and membership in the nation is questionable.

One could argue that the anchor baby rhetoric is meant to mute the political power of a vulnerable class of citizens, fostered by those who fear demographic change. So-called anchor babies might internalize the stigmatizing characterizations and demeaning practices that question their citizenship, rendering them docile and accepting of the idea that they are undeserving members of society. On the other hand, history may tell another story, one in which the objects of the anchor baby discourse feel the pain it causes them and use it to fuel their political engagement. It is too early to say with certainty which outcome will prevail, but the demographic strength, increasing education levels, and economic gains of the children of immigrants suggest they will not let the anchor baby rhetoric diminish them as people and as citizens of the United States of America.

Why does it matter that we engage with the idea of citizenship and detail the meaning of anchor babies in public discourse? Because the life of the nation should be a life examined. The children of immigrants deserve a critical and productive examination of the rhetoric and practices that can limit their participation in the nation as full-fledged Americans. The most positive outcome of putting the "anchor baby" concept under the microscope of critical review is that we exorcise it from public discourse. Rather than divisive rhetoric, we must engage in the hard work of building a nation of inclusion.

ACKNOWLEDGMENTS

First and foremost, I would like to thank Kate Wahl for her unwavering support for this project. From the beginning, Kate's encouragement and insightful suggestions on various drafts were indispensable. I am filled with gratitude for the time and effort Kate contributed to this book.

I am also indebted to the outside reviewers of the manuscript. Their suggestions and observations were incredibly helpful.

I would also like to thank Cathy Ota for her support and critical interventions when needed. For longer than I can remember she has been an informal editor of my work. Ours is a wonderful home where creativity can flourish.

Finally, I would like to thank my father- and mother-in-law, Peter and Makiko Ota. As children of Japanese immigrants they experienced the internment camps of World War II, the complete disregard for their constitutional rights as citizens, and the racial stigma of being labeled "enemy aliens." They faced these social traumas with dignity, hope, and charity. I learned from them that we cannot let ignorance deny us our humanity.

NOTES

PROLOGUE

1. "Here's Donald Trump's Presidential Announcement Speech," *Time*, June 16, 2015, http://time.com/3923128/donald-trump-announcement-speech/.

2. Alan Rappeport, "Discussing Immigration, Donald Trump and Jeb Bush Use an Offensive Term," *New York Times*, August 20, 2015.

3. Linda Bosniak, *The Citizen and the Alien: Dilemmas of Contemporary Membership* (Princeton: Princeton University Press, 2008); Patrick J. Charles, "Decoding the Fourteenth Amendment's Citizenship Clause: Unlawful Immigrants, Allegiance, Personal Subjection, and the Law," *Washburn Law Journal* 51 (2012): 211–60.

4. Mae M. Ngai, "Birthright Citizenship and the Alien Citizen," *Fordham Law Review* 75, no. 1 (2007): 2521–30.

5. Ibid.

6. Leo R. Chavez, *The Latino Threat: Constructing Citizens, Immigrants, and the Nation*, 2nd ed. (Stanford: Stanford University Press, 2013); Carmen R. Lugo-Lugo and Mary K. Bloodsworth-Lugo, "'Anchor/Terror Babies' and Latina Bodies: Immigration Rhetoric in the 21st Century and the Feminization of Terrorism," *Journal of Interdisciplinary Feminist Thought* 8, no. 1 (2014): 1–18.

7. Stephen Castles and Alastair Davidson, *Citizenship and Migration: Globalization and the Politics of Belonging* (New York: Routledge, 2000); Ngai, "Birthright Citizenship and the Alien Citizen"; Rebecca Martinez, "Sexual Assault (Threat): Policing Brown Women's Bodies on the Mexico-U.S. Border," in *Policing Black and Brown Bodies*, ed. Sandra Weissinger and Dwayne Mack (Lanham: Rowman & Littlefield, 2017).

8. "A Profile of a Lost Generation," *Los Angles Times Magazine*, December 13, 1987. For a summary of the history of the term "anchor baby," see http://en.wikipedia.org/wiki/Anchor_baby.

9. Leo R. Chavez, *Shadowed Lives: Undocumented Immigrants in American Society*, 3rd ed. (Belmont: Wadsworth, Cengage Learning, 2013).

10. Ibid., 197.

11. Michelle Malkin, "No More Drive-By Citizenship," *Michelle Malkin Blog*, June 13, 2004, http://michellemalkin.com/2004/06/13/no-more-drive-by-citizenship/.

12. "What Makes an American?," *Jewish World Review*, July 4, 2003, www.jewishworldreview.com/michelle/malkin070403.asp.

13. "Illegal alien" is the term preferred by those favoring immigration restrictions. Academics tend to use "undocumented immigrants" or "unauthorized immigrants" because they are more neutral than "illegal alien," which casts a negative connotation.

14. Linda Greenhouse, "Sins of the Parents," *New York Times*, November 30, 2011.

15. Michael Peltier, "U.S.-Born Kids of Illegal Immigrants Have Right to Florida Tuition: Judge," *Reuters*, 2012, www.reuters.com/article/us-usa-florida-universities-immigration-idUSBRE8841F020120905.

16. Michael Finnegan and Kurtis Lee, "Trump, Taunted by Protesters, Delivers Barbs on Immigration in L.A. Harbor Speech," *Los Angeles Times*, September 15, 2015.

17. *American Heritage Dictionary of the English Language*, 5th ed., s.v. "anchor baby."

18. http://ahdictionary.com/word/search.html?q=anchor+baby.

19. Nilda Flores-Gonzalez refers to U.S.-born Latinos as "citizens but not Americans." See Nilda Flores-Gonzalez, *Citizens but Not Americans: Race and Belonging among Latino Millennials* (New York: New York University Press, 2018).

CHAPTER 1

1. *U.S. News & World Report*, June 22, 1974, 30.

2. David M. Reimers, *Still the Golden Door: The Third World Comes to America* (New York: Columbia University Press, 1985); David M. Reimers, *Unwelcome Strangers: American Identity and the Turn against Immigration* (New York: Columbia University Press, 1998).

3. Migration Policy Institute, "Largest U.S. Immigrant Groups over Time, 1960–Present," 2016, www.migrationpolicy.org/programs/data-hub/charts/largest-immigrant-groups-over-time.

4. Pew Research Center, "Chapter 5: U.S. Foreign-Born Population Trends," 2015, www.pewhispanic.org/2015/09/28/chapter-5-u-s-foreign-born-population-trends/.

5. During the period between 1965 and 2015, the *New York Times* published 69 articles on anchor babies and 91 separate articles on birthright citizenship. The *Los Angeles Times* published 55 articles on anchor babies and 105 separate articles on birthright citizenship.

6. Leo R. Chavez, *Covering Immigration: Popular Images and the Politics of the Nation* (Berkeley: University of California Press, 2001).

7. Wayne King, "Mexican Women Cross Border So Babies Can Be U.S. Citizens," *New York Times*, November 21, 1982.

8. Peter H. Schuck and Rogers M. Smith, *Citizenship without Consent: Illegal Aliens in the American Polity* (New Haven: Yale University Press, 1985).

9. Bill Chappell, "Germany Deports Native-Born Terrorism Suspects, in a First," *National Public Radio*, March 22, 2017.

10. Larry Gordon, "Glendale Racial Debate to Go On," *Los Angeles Times*, June 23, 1987.

11. Quote and discussion of the Pace amendment available at https://en.wikipedia.org/wiki/William_Daniel_Johnson.

12. *U.S. News & World Report*, August 19, 1985.

13. John Tanton, quoted in Ruth Conniff, "The War on Aliens: The Right Calls the Shots," *The Progressive*, October 1993, 22–29.

14. *Time,* "Beyond the Melting Pot," April 9, 1990, 30.

15. Ibid., 31.

16. Chavez, *Latino Threat*, 87–88.

17. Daryl Kelley, "Gallegly Urges Stricter Rules for Citizenship," *Los Angeles Times*, October 24, 1991.

18. Santiago O'Donnell, "Angry Latino Leaders Decry Gallegly Proposal," *Los Angeles Times*, October 26, 1991, B 5.

19. Jack Cheevers, "Protest Targets Gallegly Legislation," *Los Angeles Times*, November 28, 1991.

20. Kay Saillant and Alan C. Miller, "Gallegly Appointed to Judiciary Panel," *Los Angeles Times*, December 12, 1992.

21. California Ballot Pamphlet 1992, http://repository.uchastings .edu/ca_ballot_props/1091/; see also Philip Martin, "Proposition 187 in California," *International Migration Review* 24 (1995): 255–63; Michael A. Olivas, "Storytelling out of School: Undocumented College Residency, Race, and Reaction," *Hastings Constitutional Law Quarterly* 22 (1995): 1019–86; Kevin R. Johnson, "Public Benefits and Immigration: The Intersection of Immigration Status, Ethnicity, Gender, and Class," *UCLA Law Review* 42, no. 6 (1995): 1509–75.

22. Although Proposition 187 passed with 67 percent of the vote in 1992, seven years later, in September 1999, a U.S. district judge issued a final ruling that essentially scrapped the proposition. "Judge's Final Ruling Scraps Proposition 187," *Los Angeles Times*, September 14, 1999. Proposition 187 was a forerunner of later "get tough"-on-immigration laws in Arizona, Alabama, Georgia, Indiana, South Carolina, and Utah.

23. Bette Hammond, quoted in Elizabeth Kadetsky, "'Save Our State' Initiative: Bashing Illegals in California," *The Nation*, October 17, 1994, 418.

24. Patrick J. McDonnell, "Wilson Urges Stiff Penalties to Deter Illegal Immigrants," *Los Angeles Times*, August 10, 1993.

25. "Seeking to Deny Citizenship to Some," *New York Times*, August 11, 1993.

26. Patrick J. McDonnell and Bill Stall, "Many Obstacles to Wilson Plan on Immigration," *Los Angeles Times*, August 11, 1993.

27. "Judge Halts California Cutoff of Prenatal Care to Illegal Aliens," *New York Times*, November 28, 1996.

28. Senate Bill 1351, www.congress.gov/bill/103rd-congress/senate-bill/1351.

29. Lukas Pleva, "Reid Bashed Republicans for a Position on Immigration That He Once Pushed," *PolitiFact*, August 25, 2010, www.politifact.com/truth-o-meter/statements/2010/aug/25/harry-reid/reid-bashes-republicans-position-immigration-he-on/.

30. Ibid.

31. Neil A. Lewis, "Bill Seeks to End Automatic Citizenship for All Born in the U.S.," *New York Times*, December 14, 1995, A26.

32. Ibid.

33. "The 1996 Republican Party Platform," 1996, www.cnn.com/ALLPOLITICS/1996/conventions/san.diego/facts/gop.platform/platform.all.shtml; "GOP Convention '96; GOP Platform," *Los Angeles Times*, August 13, 1996.

34. Peter M. Warren, "Chung Won't Blend into Melting Pot," *Los Angeles Times*, August 11, 1996.

35. Frank Bruni, "Dole Rejects a Party Plank," *New York Times*, August 24, 1996.

36. Robert Pear, "Citizenship Proposal Faces Obstacle in the Constitution," *New York Times*, August 7, 1996.

37. A. M. Rosenthal, "Dred Scott in San Diego," *New York Times*, August 9, 1996.

38. "A Contradictory Message Resounds in San Diego; Inclusion and Intolerance Walk Together at GOP Convention," *Los Angeles Times*, August 14, 1996.

39. Patrick J. McDonnell, "U.S. Citizenship Rules More Liberal Than Most," *Los Angeles Times*, July 4, 1997.

40. Gebe Martinez, "Immigrants' Rights Bills Create Strong Debate," *Los Angeles Times*, June 26, 1997.

41. Ibid.

42. Leo R. Chavez, "Culture Change and Cultural Reproduction: Lessons from Research on Transnational Migration," in *Globalization and Change in Fifteen Cultures: Born in One World and Living in Another*, ed. Janice Stockard and George Spindler (Belmont: Thomson-Wadsworth, 2006), 283–303; Douglas S. Massey and Karen A. Pren, "Unintended Consequences of US Immigration Policy: Explaining the Post-1965 Surge from Latin America," *Population and Development Review* 38, no. 1 (2012): 1–29.

43. Jeffrey S. Passel, "Unauthorized Migrants: Numbers and Characteristics" (Washington, DC: Pew Hispanic Center, 2005); Jeffrey S. Passel and D'Vera Cohn, "Unauthorized Immigrant Population: National and State Trends, 2010" (Washington, DC: Pew Hispanic Center, 2011), http://pewhispanic.org/reports/report.php?ReportID=133; Robinson J. Gregory, "ESCAP II: Demographic Analysis Results" (Washington, DC: U.S. Department of Commerce, Bureau of the Census, 2001).

44. Elizabeth Grieco, "The Foreign Born from Mexico in the United States" (Washington, DC: Migration Policy Institute, 2003); Jeffrey Passel and D'Vera Cohn, "Number of Babies Born to Unauthorized Immigrants in U.S. Continues to Decline" (Washington, DC: Pew Research Center, 2016); David C. Griffith, "Rural Industry and Mexican Immigration and Settlement in North Carolina," in *New Destinations: Mexican Immigration in the United States*, ed. Victor Zuniga and Ruben Hernandez-Leon (New York: Russell Sage Foundation, 2005), 50–75; Helen B. Marrow, *New Destination Dreaming: Immigration, Race, and Legal*

Status in the Rural American South (Stanford: Stanford University Press, 2011); Aaron Terrazas, "Immigrants in New-Destination States" (Washington, DC: Migration Policy Institute, 2011), www.migrationinformation.org/USFocus/display.cfm?ID=826; Victor Zuniga and Ruben Hernandez-Leon, eds., *New Destinations: Mexican Immigration in the United States* (New York: Russell Sage Foundation., 2005).

45. Angela Stuesse, *Scratching out a Living: Latinos, Race, and Work in the Deep South* (Berkeley: University of California Press, 2016).

46. Samuel P. Huntington, "The Special Case of Mexican Immigration: Why Mexico Is a Problem," *The American Enterprise*, December 2000, 22.

47. George W. Bush, "The National Security Strategy of the United States of America," White House, Washington, DC, www.whitehouse.gov/ncs.html.

48. Leti Volpp, "The Citizen and the Terrorist," *UCLA Law Review* 49 (2002): 1575–1600.

49. Samuel P. Huntington, "The Hispanic Challenge," *Foreign Policy*, March/April 2004, 32.

50. Patrick J. McDonnell, "Brash Evangelist," *Los Angeles Times*, July 15, 2001.

51. Ibid.

52. Ibid.

53. For Lou Dobbs's comments and a discussion of anchor babies and the efforts to repeal the Fourteenth Amendment and birthright citizenship, see *Lou Dobbs Tonight*, April 15, 2006, www.youtube.com/watch?v=o6x1t8ej-Tk.

54. Barbara Demick, "The Baby Registry of Choice; Thousands of Pregnant South Koreans Travel to the U.S. to Give Birth to American Citizens," *Los Angeles Times*, June 12, 2002.

55. Anna Gorman, "Affluent Cross Border to U.S. for Childbirth," *Los Angeles Times*, April 17, 2003.

56. Ibid.

57. Nina Bernstein, "A Mexican Baby Boom in New York Shows the Strength of a New Immigrant Group," *New York Times*, June 4, 2007.

58. "Record Immigration Is Changing the Face of New York's Neighborhoods," *New York Times*, January 24, 2005.

59. HR 698, Citizenship Reform Act of 2005, www.congress .gov/bill/109th-congress/house-bill/698.

60. Warren Vieth, "GOP Faction Wants to Change 'Birthright Citizenship' Policy," *Los Angeles Times*, December 10, 2005.

61. Women have historically been suspect when arriving as immigrants due to issues of sexuality, moral turpitude, and use of social services for themselves and their children. See Eithne Luib-héid, *Entry Denied: Controlling Sexuality at the Border* (Minneapolis: University of Minnesota Press, 2002).

62. Lizette Alvarez and John M. Broder, "More and More, Women Risk All to Enter U.S.," *New York Times*, January 10, 2006.

63. Ibid.

64. Chavez, *Latino Threat*; Bill Ong Hing and Kevin R. Johnson, "The Immigrant Rights Marches of 2006 and the Prospects for a New Civil Rights Movement," *Harvard Civil Rights-Civil Liberties Law Review* 42, no. 1 (2007): 99–138; Kim Voss and Irene Bloemraad, *Rallying for Immigrant Rights: The Fight for Inclusion in 21st Century America* (Berkeley: University of California Press, 2011).

65. Julia Preston, "Texas Hospitals Reflect Debate on Immigration," *New York Times*, July 18, 2006.

66. Ibid.

67. Rachel L. Swarns, "In Georgia, Immigrants Unsettle Old Sense of Place," *New York Times*, August 4, 2005.

68. Nina Bernstein, "First-Baby Sweepstakes Fuels Immigration Baby Debate," *New York Times*, January 6, 2007.

69. Bill Plaschke, "From Humble Beginnings, an American Dream," *Los Angeles Times*, August 20, 2008.

70. "Henry Cejudo's Road to Glory," *Los Angeles Times*, August 24, 2008.

71. Julia Preston, "Citizenship from Birth Is Challenged on the Right," *New York Times*, August 6, 2010.

72. "Immigration Hardball," *New York Times*, November 14, 2010.

73. Tim Rutten, "Obama Needs to Step Up," *Los Angeles Times*, May 28, 2010.

74. "Xenophobia: Fear-Mongering for American Votes," *New York Times*, August 5, 2010.

75. Teresa Watanabe, "Aid Figures Cause Alarm; Antonovic Calls for Change as Payments to Children of Illegal Immigrants Increase," *Los Angeles Times*, September 6, 2010.

76. Arizona's Senate Bill 1070 is available at www.azleg.gov/legtext/49leg/2r/bills/sb1070s.pdf.

77. Rutten, "Obama Needs to Step Up."

78. Julia Preston, "Political Battle on Illegal Immigration Shifts to States," *New York Times*, December 31, 2010.

79. Andy Barr, "Graham Eyes 'Birthright Citizenship,'" *Politco*, July 29, 2010, www.politico.com/news/stories/0710/40395.html #ixzz0v5pFRNr4; Eve Conant, "The Next Front on Immigration," *Newsweek*, August 9, 2010.

80. Otto Santa Ana, "'Like an Animal I Was Treated': Anti-Immigrant Metaphors in US Public Discourse," *Discourse and Society* 10, no. 2 (1996): 192–224.

81. Peter H. Schuck, "Birthright of a Nation," *New York Times*, August 16, 2010.

82. Gregory Rodriguez, "A Broader View of the 14th Amendment," *Los Angeles Times*, August 16, 2010.

83. Marc Lacey, "Birthright Citizenship Looms as Next Immigration Battle," *New York Times*, January 4, 2011.

84. Patrick J. Buchanan, *Suicide of a Superpower: Will America Survive to 2025?* (New York: St. Martin's Press, 2011), 422.

85. Ibid., 142.

86. Patrick J. Buchanan, *State of Emergency: The Third World Invasion and Conquest of America* (New York: St. Martins Press, 2006), 132.

87. Julia Preston, "State Lawmakers Outline Plans to End Birthright Citizenship, Drawing Outcry," *New York Times*, January 5, 2011.

88. Ibid.

89. "Angry Arizona, Again," *New York Times*, February 26, 2011.

90. Jennifer Medina, "Arriving as Pregnant Tourists, Leaving with American Babies," *New York Times*, March 28, 2011.

91. Flora Lee Peir, "In Queens, New Mothers and Old Asian Custom," *New York Times*, June 3, 2011.

92. Medina, "Arriving as Pregnant Tourists, Leaving with American Babies."

93. Ibid.

94. Julia Preston, "Births Are Outpacing Immigration for Mexican-Americans, Report Says," *New York Times*, July 14, 2011.

95. Susan Saulny, "Hispanic Pregnancies Fall in U.S. as Women Choose Smaller Families," *New York Times*, December 31, 2012.

96. "G.O.P. Candidates Follow Trump to the Bottom on Immigration," *New York Times*, August 20, 2015.

97. Nick Corasaniti, "Donald Trump Releases Plan to Combat Illegal Immigration," *New York Times*, August 16, 2015.

98. "Trump: Deport Children of Immigrants Living Illegally in U.S.," *Los Angeles Times*, August 17, 2015.

99. The *National Review* ran an article supporting changing the Fourteenth Amendment at this time: John C. Eastman, "We Can Apply the 14th Amendment While Also Reforming Birthright Citizenship," *National Review*, August 24, 2015, www.national review.com/article/422960/birthright-citizenship-reform-it-without -repealing-14th-amendment.

100. Julia Preston and Trip Gabriel, "Donald Trump Paints Republicans into Corner with Hispanics," *New York Times*, August

18, 2015; "G.O.P. Candidates Follow Trump to the Bottom on Immigration"; Kate Linthicum, "As Debate Highlights GOP Divide on Immigration, White House Woos New Citizens," *Los Angeles Times*, September 17, 2015.

101. Seema Mehta, "Attacks Are a Good Sign for Fiorina," *Los Angeles Times*, September 3, 2015; David Rivkin and John Yoo, "Ignore Trump—The Issue of Birthright Citizenship Has Been Settled," *Los Angeles Times*, September 6, 2015.

102. Ashley Parker, "Dropping Mild Tone, Jeb Bush Assails Donald Trump as Leaning Democratic," *The New York Times*, August 20, 2015.

103. Noah Bierman, "Donald Trump Says the Wall He'll Build on the Border Could Bear His Name," *Los Angeles Times*, August 19, 2015.

104. Rappeport, "Discussing Immigration, Donald Trump and Jeb Bush Use an Offensive Term."

105. "Jeb Bush's Choice of Words Upsets Asian-Americans," *New York Times*, August 25, 2015.

106. "Jeb Bush Falls into a Trap," *New York Times*, August 25, 2015.

107. David Lauter, "Polarization on Immigration Rising," *Los Angeles Times*, October 11, 2015; Lisa Mascaro, "From Barry Goldwater to Pete Wilson to Donald Trump: Is GOP on Verge of Losing Latinos for a Generation?," *Los Angeles Times*, June 12, 2016; Kate Linthicum, "An Immigration Dilemma; Taking Hard Line Now May Cost Candidates Latino Votes Later," *Los Angeles Times*, September 18, 2015.

108. Michael Finnegan and Kurtis Lee, "Cheers, Jeers Greet Trump," *Los Angeles Times*, September 16, 2015; "'Disgusted' Police Condemn Violent Protesters at Donald Trump Rally in San Jose," *Los Angeles Times,* June 3, 2016; Kate Linthicum, "Going to Bat for Immigrants," *Los Angeles Times*, September 17, 2015.

109. Eva Millona and Joshua Hoyt, "A Deeper Debate on Immigration Is Welcome," *Los Angeles Times*, September 14, 2015.

110. Emily Bazelon, "Department of Justification," *New York Times Magazine*, March 5, 2017.

111. www.numbersusa.com/print/news/rep-steve-king-reintroduces-bill-end-birthright-citizenship.

112. Theodore Schleifer, "King Doubles Down on Controversial 'Babies' Tweet," *CNN Politics*, March 14, 2017, www.cnn.com/2017/03/13/politics/steve-king-babies-tweet-cnntv/index.html.

113. Nicholas Kulish, "With Ally in Oval Office, Immigration Hard-Liners Ascend to Power," *New York Times*, April 24, 2017. For Feere's views on birthright citizenship, see Jon D. Feere, *Birthright Citizenship in the United States: A Global Comparison* (Washington, DC: Center for Migration Studies, 2010).

114. Jeff Landa, "Initiative Idea Echoes Prop. 187," *Los Angeles Times*, April 10, 2017.

115. Passel and Cohn, "Number of Babies Born to Unauthorized Immigrants in U.S. Continues to Decline."

116. As Michel Foucault noted about discourse and power: "We must cease once and for all to describe the effects of power in negative terms: it 'excludes,' it 'represses,' it 'censors,' it 'abstracts,' it 'masks,' it 'conceals.' In fact power produces; it produces reality; it produces domains of objects and rituals of truth. The individual and the knowledge that may be gained of him belong to this production." Michel Foucault, *Discipline and Punish* (London: Tavistock, 1977), 194.

117. For examples of the ways media frame events, see R. Benford and David Snow, "Framing Processes and Social Movements: An Overview and Assessment," *Annual Review of Sociology* 26 (2000): 611–39; Titus Ensink and Christoph Sauer, "Social-Functional and Cognitive Approaches to Discourse Interpretation: The Role of Frame and Perspective," in *Framing and Perspectivising in Discourse*, ed. Titus Ensink and Christoph Sauer (Philadelphia: John Benjamins, 2003), 1–21; Knud S. Larsen et al., "Threat Perception and Attitudes toward Documented and Undocumented Immigrants in the United States: Framing the Debate and Con-

flict Resolution," *European Journal of Social Sciences* 7, no. 4 (2009): 115–34; Daniel B. German, "The Role of the Media in Political Socialization and Attitude Formation toward Racial/Ethnic Minorities in the US," in *Nationalism, Ethnicity, and Identity*, ed. Russell F. Farnen (New Brunswick: Transaction, 1994); Susan Bibler Coutin and Phyllis Pease Chock, "'Your Friend, the Illegal': Definition and Paradox in Newspaper Accounts of U.S. Immigration Reform," *Identities* 2 (1995): 123–48.

118. As Lakoff, Dean, and Hazen noted: "Metaphors repeated often enough eventually become part of your physical brain. Use the word 'illegal' often enough, which suggests criminal, which suggests immoral, and you have framed the issue of immigration to a remarkable degree." George Lakoff, Howard Dean, and Don Hazen, *Don't Think of an Elephant! Know Your Values and Frame the Debate—The Essential Guide for Progressives* (White River Junction: Chelsea Green, 2004).

CHAPTER 2

1. Neal Katyal and Paul Clement, "On the Meaning of 'Natural Born Citizen,'" *Harvard Law Review* 128, no. 5 (2015): 161–64.

2. Ibid.

3. Ibid.

4. Wiliam Rawle, *A View of the Constitution of the United States of America* (Philadelphia: Philip H. Nicklin Law Bookseller, 1829).

5. "U.S. Supreme Court: Inglis v. Trustees of Sailor's Snug Harbor, 28 U.S. 99 (1830)," Justia.com, http://supreme.justia.com/us/28/99/case.html.

6. William L. Marcy, "Native Sons of Alien Parents," *New York Times*, March 20, 1854.

7. Jus soli is common to most countries in the Americas and Caribbean. But other countries also practice jus soli, for example Pakistan, Fiji, and Lesotho.

8. Jennifer L. Hochschild and John H. Mollenkopf, eds., *Bringing Outsiders In: Transatlantic Perspectives on Immigrant Political Incorporation* (Ithaca: Cornell University Press, 2009).

9. Countries with a modified jus soli include the United Kingdom, Australia, New Zealand, South Africa, France, and Germany. See Library of Congress, "Citizenship Based on Birth in Country," www.loc.gov/law/help/citizenship-birth-country/index.php.

10. To be Chinese, Japanese, or Saudi, for example, one must have Chinese, Japanese, or Saudi blood through a parent. Almost all countries allow citizenship through blood but many restrict or limit citizenship by birth. The large numbers of women working as migrant laborers often encounter problems with their children's citizenship in countries that do not confer birthright citizenship or that require the father to formally acknowledge the child as his. Nicole Constable, *Born out of Place: Migrant Mothers and the Politics of International Labor* (Berkeley: University of California Press, 2014).

11. Anwen Tormey, "Everyone with Eyes Can See the Problem": Moral Citizens and the Space of Irish Nationhood," *International Migration* 45, no. 3 (2007): 69–100; Erin Moran, "Immigrant Appearances and the Emergence of 'Active Citizenship' in Ireland" (paper presented at the annual meetings of the American Anthropological Association, Washington, DC, November 30, 2007); Eithne Luibhéid, *Pregnant on Arrival: Making the Illegal Immigrant* (Minneapolis: University of Minnesota Press, 2013). Countries that do not have birthright citizenship have experienced "dragging economies, new forms of fraud, a disenfranchised underclass, and children deported to places they have never even visited." Julie M. Weise, "Citizen Who?," *Los Angeles Times*, September 2, 2010.

12. Jerome R. Adams, *Greasers and Gringos: The Historical Roots of Anglo-Hispanic Prejudice* (Jefferson, NC: McFarland, 2006); A. De Leon, *They Called Them Greasers* (Austin: University of Texas Press, 1983).

13. Richard Griswold del Castillo, *The Treaty of Guadalupe Hidalgo: A Legacy of Conflict* (Norman: University of Oklahoma Press, 1990).

14. Later, however, Mexican Americans would be subject to similar Jim Crow practices and school segregation as experienced by other nonwhite Americans. Tara J. Yosso et al., "From Jim Crow to Affirmative Action and Back Again: A Critical Race Discussion of Racialized Rationales and Access to Higher Education," *Review of Research in Education* 28 (2004): 1–25.

15. http://caselaw.1p.findlaw.com/data/constitution/amendment14/.

16. Anna Pegler-Gordon, *In Sight of America: Photography and the Development of U.S. Immigration Policy* (Berkeley: University of California Press, 2009).

17. As Ngai notes, "The anti-Chinese nativists understood that granting citizenship to the children of Chinese assured permanent settlement and an accretion of the Chinese population, thereby undermining the very objectives of exclusion." Although the lower courts decided some cases in favor of U.S.-Chinese persons, such as Look Tin Sing, it was not until the U.S. Supreme Court case of Wong Kim Ark that the birthright issue was settled. Ngai, "Birthright Citizenship and the Alien Citizen," 2528. Natalia Molina, *How Race Is Made in America: Immigration, Citizenship, and the Historical Power of Racial Scripts* (Berkeley: University of California, Press, 2014).

18. U.S. Supreme Court, "United States v. Wong Kim Ark," in 169 U.S. 649 (Cornell University Law School, Legal Information Institute, 1898).

19. Ibid. The discussion of the Wong Kim Ark case in this section comes primarily from the actual published Supreme Court decision.

20. "US Supreme Court: United States v. Wong Kim Ark, 169 U.S. 649 (1898)," Justia.com, http://supreme.justia.com/us/169/649/case.html#715. See also http://en.wikipedia.org/wiki/Wong_Kim_Ark.

21. Gary Gerstle, *American Crucible: Race and Nation in the Twentieth Century* (Princeton: Princeton University Press, 2001), 115.

22. Cited in U.S. Supreme Court, "United States v. Wong Kim Ark."

23. Rita J. Simon, *Public Opinion and the Immigrant* (Lexington: Lexington Books, 1985), 186.

24. Dorothy E. Roberts, "Who May Give Birth to Citizens? Reproduction, Eugenics, and Immigration," in *Immigrants Out! The New Nativism and the Anti-immigrant Impulse in the United States*, ed. Juan F. Perea (New York: New York University Press, 1997), 212.

25. "Phelan Would Deny Citizenship to All Japanese Born in America," *Los Angeles Times*, January 22, 1920, 11.

26. "Japs Win in Court Ruling," *Los Angeles Times*, May 2, 1922, 11.

27. Myra Nye, "Alien Blow Defeated: Anticitizenship Move Fails," *Los Angeles Times*, April 25, 1931.

28. "Curb Advised on Citizenship," *Los Angeles Times*, April 12, 1941, A1.

29. "Jury Indorses Jap Farm Ban," *Los Angeles Times*, December 10, 1942, 22.

30. *Plyler v. Doe*, 457 U.S. 202 (no. 80-1538), Legal Information Institute, www.law.cornell.edu/supremecourt/text/457/202.

CHAPTER 3

1. "Editorial: Can You Be Born in Texas and Not Be an American?," *Los Angeles Times*, October 29, 2015.

2. Molly Hennessy-Fiske, "Immigrants Sue Texas over State's Denial of Birth Certificates for U.S.-Born Children, *Los Angeles Times*, July 18, 2015.

3. Ibid.

4. Julia Preston, "Lawsuit Forces Texas to Make It Easier for Immigrants to Get Birth Certificates," *New York Times*, July 24, 2016.

5. Manny Fernandez, "Immigrants Fight Texas' Birth Certificate Rules," *New York Times*, September 17, 2015.

6. Plaintiffs' Emergency Application for Preliminary Injunction, Maria Isabel Perales Serna, et al., Plaintiffs v. Texas Department of State Health Services, Vital Statistics Unit, et al., Defendants (2015).

7. Order: Maria Isabel Perales Serna, et al., Plaintiffs v. Texas Department of State Health Services, Vital Statistics Unit, et al., Defendants (2015).

8. Ibid., 9.

9. Ibid., 12.

10. Molly Hennessy-Fiske, "Agreement on Birth Certificates," *Los Angeles Times*, July 26, 2016; Preston, "Lawsuit Forces Texas to Make It Easier for Immigrants to Get Birth Certificates."

11. Cited in Hennessy-Fiske, "Agreement on Birth Certificates."

12. Cited in Preston, "Lawsuit Forces Texas to Make It Easier for Immigrants to Get Birth Certificates."

13. Cecilia Menjivar and Leisy J. Abrego, "Legal Violence: Immigration Law and the Lives of Central American Immigrants," *American Journal of Sociology* 117, no. 5 (2012): 1380–1421.

14. Affidavits Document 25-1, Maria Isabel Perales Serna, et al., Plaintiffs v. Texas Department of State Health Services, Vital Statistics Unit, et al., Defendants. The plaintiffs' actual first names are used here.

15. Anh Do et al., "After a Waiter's Demand for 'Proof of Residency,' Familiar Echoes of Discrimination Take on a New Resonance," *Los Angeles Times*, March 21, 2017.

16. Amy Johnson, "Vandal Spray Paints 'Illegal' on Man's Van, but It Didn't Dawn on Him It Was Possible Hate Crime," *CBS Los Angeles*, March 2, 2017.

17.   Deborah A. Boehm, *Returned: Going and Coming in an Age of Deportation* (Berkeley: University of California Press, 2016).

18.   Timothy J. Dunn, *The Militarization of the U.S.-Mexico Border, 1978–1992: Low-Intensity Conflict Doctrine Comes Home* (Austin: Center for Mexican American Studies Books, 1996); Timothy J. Dunn, "Military Collaboration with the Border Patrol in the U.S.-Mexico Border Region: Inter-organizational Relations and Human Rights Implications," *Journal of Political and Military Sociology* 27 (1999): 257–77; Peter Andreas, *Border Games: Policing the U.S.-Mexico Divide* (Ithaca: Cornell University Press, 2000); Jonathan X. Inda, *Targeting Immigrants: Government, Technology, and Ethics* (Malden: Blackwell, 2006).

19.   Douglas S. Massey, Jorge Durand, and Nolan J. Malone, *Beyond Smoke and Mirrors: Mexican Immigration in an Era of Economic Integration* (New York: Russell Sage Foundation, 2002); Wayne A. Cornelius, "Death at the Border: Efficacy and Unintended Consequences of US Immigration Control Policy," *Population and Development Review* 27, no. 4 (2001): 661–85; "Illegal Immigration: Border-Crossing Deaths Have Doubled since 1995" (Washington, DC: U.S. Government Accountability Office, 2006); Border Patrol's Efforts to Prevent Deaths Have Not Been Fully Evaluated" (Washington, DC: U.S. Government Accountability Office, 2006).

20.   Chavez, *Shadowed Lives.*

21.   Massey and Pren, "Unintended Consequences of US Immigration Policy."

22.   Andy Selepak, "$6 Billion a Year for Mexican 'Anchor Babies'?," *Accuracy in Media* (2007), www.aim.org/special-report/6-billion-a-year-for-mexican-anchor-babies/.

23.   Jeffrey S. Passel and D'Vera Cohn, "A Portrait of Unauthorized Immigrants in the United States" (Washington, DC: Pew Hispanic Center, 2009).

24.   Passel and Cohn, "Number of Babies Born to Unauthorized Immigrants in U.S. Continues to Decline"; Robert Warren

and Donald Kerwin, "Mass Deportations Would Impoverish US Families and Create Immense Social Costs," *Journal on Migration and Human Security* 5, no. 1 (2017): 1–8.

25. Chavez, *Shadowed Lives*.

26. Ibid., 186.

27. Karell Roxas, "My Secret Life as an Undocumented Immigrant," *Elle*, March 10, 2017.

28. Abraham Hoffman, *Unwanted Americans: Mexican Americans in the Great Depression, Repatriation Pressures, 1929–1939* (Tucson: University of Arizona Press, 1974).

29. The Lemon Grove Incident, http://espinosaproductions.com/project/the-lemon-grove-incident/.

30. Susan Bibler Coutin, "Place and Presence within Salvadoran Deportees' Narratives of Removal," *Childhood* 20, no. 3 (2013): 323–36; Susan Bibler Coutin, "Deportation Studies: Origins, Themes and Directions," *Journal of Ethnic and Migration Studies* 41, no. 4 (2014): 671–81; Nathalie Peutz, "Embarking on an Anthropology of Removal," *Current Anthropology* 47, no. 2 (2006): 217–41; Veronica Montes, "The Role of Emotions in the Construction of Masculinity: Guatemalan Migrant Men, Transnational Migration, and Family Relations," *Gender and Society* 27, no. 4 (2013): 469–90; Randy Capps et al., *Paying the Price: The Impact of Immigration Raids on America's Children* (Washington, DC: National Council of La Raza and the Urban Institute, 2007); Beth F. Baker, "Impacts of Deportation: Perspectives from Latin America and the United States," *Practicing Anthropology* 38, no. 1 (2016): 34–35.

31. Passel and Cohn, "Unauthorized Immigrant Population."

32. Joanna Dreby, "The Burden of Deportation on Children in Mexican Immigrant Families," *Journal of Marriage and Family* 74 (2012); Joanna Dreby, *Everyday Illegal: When Policies Undermine Immigrant Families* (Berkeley: University of California Press, 2015); Jacqueline María Hagan, Nestor Rodriguez, and Brianna Castro, "Social Effects of Mass Deportations by the United States

Government, 2000–2010," *Ethnic and Racial Studies* 34, no. 8 (2011): 1374–91; Laura E. Enriquez, "Multigenerational Punishment: Shared Experiences of Undocumented Immigration Status within Mixed-Status Families," *Journal of Marriage and Family* 77, no. 4 (2015): 939–53.

33. Massey, Durand, and Malone, *Beyond Smoke and Mirrors.*

34. Philip Martin, "Mexico-US Migration," in *NAFTA Revisited: Achievements and Challenges*, ed. Gary Hufbauer and Jeffrey Schott (Washington, DC: Institute for International Economics, 2005), 441–86.

35. Lisa Mascaro, "Deportations Revive Rift between Obama and Fellow Democrats," *Los Angeles Times*, January 9, 2016.

36. Randy Capps et al., "Implications of Immigration Enforcement Activities for the Well-Being of Children of Immigrant Families: A Review of the Literature" (Washington, DC: Urban Institute and Migration Policy Institute, 2015).

37. "Border Enforcement Policies Ensnare Parents of US Citizen Children," Human Rights Watch, January 8, 2015, www.hrw .org/news/2015/01/08/border-enforcement-policies-ensnare-parents -us-citizen-children.

38. Donald J. Trump, "Executive Order: Enhancing Public Safety in the Interior of the United States," January 25, 2017.

39. Nicholas Kulish, Caitlin Dickerson, and Ron Nixon, "Immigration Agents Discover a New Freedom on Deportations," *New York Times*, February 25, 2017.

40. Nigel Duara et al., "This Is How Trump's Expanded Deportation Policy Is Bering Felt across the U.S.," *Los Angeles Times*, February 22, 2017; Monica Davey, "He's a Local Pillar in a Trump Town. Now He Could Be Deported," *New York Times*, February 27, 2017; Matt Pearce and Kurtis Lee, "Federal Immigration Agents Arrest a DACA-Eligible 'Dreamer' near Scattle, Lawsuit Says," *Los Angeles Times*, February 14, 2017; Doug Smith, "Los Angeles Officials Urge ICE Agents to Stop Identifying Themselves as Police," *Los Angeles Times*, February 23, 2017.

41. Warren and Kerwin, "Mass Deportations Would Impoverish US Families."

42. Sherry B. Ortner, "Subjectivity and Cultural Critique," *Anthropological Theory* 5, no. 1 (2005): 31–52; Veena Das et al., *Violence and Subjectivity* (Berkeley: University of California Press, 2000); Cassaundra Rodriguez, "Experiencing 'Illegality' as a Family? Immigration Enforcement, Social Policies, and Discourses Targeting Mexican Mixed-Status Families," *Sociology Compass* 10, no. 8 (2016): 706–17; Ruth Gomberg-Munoz, *Becoming Legal: Immigration Law and Mixed-Status Families* (Oxford: Oxford University Press, 2017).

43. Judith Butler, *Gender Trouble: Feminism and the Subversion of Identity* (New York: Routledge, 1999).

44. Sarah S. Willen, "Toward a Critical Phenomenology of 'Illegality': State Power, Criminality and Abjectivity among Undocumented Migrant Workers in Tel Aviv, Israel," *International Migration* 45, no. 3 (2007): 8–38; Roberto G. Gonzales and Leo R Chavez, "'Awakening to a Nightmare': Abjectivity and Illegality in the Lives of Undocumented 1.5 Generation Latino Immigrants in the United States," *Current Anthropology* 53, no. 3 (2012): 255–81.

45. Susan Bibler Coutin, *Exiled Home: Salvadoran Transnational Youth in the Aftermath of Violence (Global Insecurities)* (Durham: Duke University Press, 2016).

46. Chris Hedges, "Deportation, and Family Ruin; Immigrant Breadwinners Are Held Far Away for Years," *New York Times*, January 1, 2001.

47. Sam Dolnick, "U.S. Returns Young Girl, a Citizen to Guatemala," *New York Times*, March 22, 2011.

48. Seth Freed Wessler, "Shattered Families: The Perilous Intersection of Immigration Enforcement and the Child Welfare System" (New York: Applied Research Center, 2011).

49. Dreby, "Burden of Deportation on Children in Mexican Immigrant Families"; Dreby, *Everyday Illegal*; Monisha Das Gupta, "'Don't Deport Our Daddies': Gendering State Deportation

Practices and Immigrant Organizing," *Gender and Society* 28, no. 1 (2013): 83–109.

50. Hedges, "Deportations and Family Ruin."

51. For a discussion of "deportability," see Nicholas De Genova, "Deportation Regime: Sovereignty, Space, and the Freedom of Movement," in *The Deportation Regime: Sovereignty, Space, and the Freedom of Movement*, ed. Nicholas De Genova and Nathalie Peutz (Durham: Duke University Press, 2010), 33–65. Nina Bernstein, "Caught between Parents and the Law," *New York Times*, February 17, 2005.

52. De Genova, "Deportation Regime"; Ruben Vives et al., "Anxiety Builds as Fears of Deportation Come to Fore," *Los Angeles Times*, February 23, 2017.

53. Joy Resmovits, "Failing to Apply for College Aid," *Los Angeles Times*, February 23, 2017, B1.

54. Anna Gorman, "The Great Divide of Citizenship," *Los Angeles Times*, May 7, 2006.

55. Ibid.

56. Ibid.

57. Richard Fausset, "Could He Be a Good American?," *Los Angeles Times*, June 11, 2011.

58. Teresa Watanabe, "Struggling Iraq Vet May Lose His Anchor," *Los Angeles Times*, October 26, 2009.

59. Steve Lopez, "Young Advocate Seeks Pope's Aid on Immigration," *Los Angeles Times*, March 22, 2014.

60. Daniel Kanstroom, "Deportation, Social Control, and Punishment: Some Thoughts about Why Hard Laws Make Bad Cases," *Harvard Law Review* 113, no. 8 (2000): 1890–1935.

61. Julia Preston, "As Deportation Pace Rises, Illegal Immigrants Dig In," *New York Times*, May 1, 2007.

62. Anna Gorman, "A Family's Painful Split Decision," *Los Angeles Times*, April 27, 2007.

63. Ibid.

64. Richard Marosi, "Building a House for His Family, but Father Can't Live in It," *Los Angeles Times*, September 20, 2013.

65. Diane Guerrero and Michelle Burford, *In the Country We Love* (New York: Henry Holt, 2016), 1–2.

66. Ibid.

67. Cecilia Menjívar and Leisy Abrego refer to these normalized and cumulative injurious effects of the law as a form of legal violence. Menjívar and Abrego, "Legal Violence," 102.

68. Hirokazu Yoshikawa has found that deporting parents can even have lasting cognitive effects on their children, including U.S. citizens. See Hirokazu Yoshikawa, *Immigrants Raising Citizens: Undocumented Parents and Their Young Children* (New York: Russell Sage Foundation, 2011); Hirokazu Yoshikawa and Ariel Kalil, "The Effects of Parental Undocumented Status on the Developmental Contexts of Young Children in Immigrant Families," *Child Development Perspectives* 5, no. 4 (2011): 291–97.

69. U.S. Citizenship and Immigration Services, "You May Be Able to Request DAPA" (Washington, DC: U.S. Department of Homeland Security, 2015).

70. Robert Warren and Donald Kerwin, "Beyond DAPA and DACA: Revisiting Legislative Reform in Light of Long-Term Trends in Unauthorized Immigration to the United States," *Journal of Migration and Human Security* 3, no. 1 (2015): 80–108.

71. Cindy Carcamo et al., "Obama Immigration Plan Hits a Deadlock," *Los Angeles Times*, June 24, 2016.

EPILOGUE

1. Cindy Carcamo et al., "Obama Immigration Plan Hits a Deadlock," *Los Angeles Times*, June 24, 2016; "Trump Rescinds Obama-Era Policy Protecting Parents of 'Anchor Babies,'" *2ANEWS*, June 16, 2017, https://2anews.us/illegal-immigration/2017/06/16/trump-rescinds-obama-era-policy-protecting-parents-anchor-babies/.

2. Giorgio Agamben refers to this as states of exception. Patricia Zavella, *I'm Neither Here nor There: Mexicans' Quotidian Struggles with Migration and Poverty* (Durham: Duke University Press, 2011).

3. Giorgio Agamben, *State of Exception* (Chicago: University of Chicago Press, 2005).

4. The study is titled "Immigration Discourse's Effect on Psychological Health and Identity"; Leo R. Chavez, Belinda Campos, Daina Sanchez, Karina Corona, and Catherine Belyeu Ruiz (University of California, Irvine, 2016).

5. Douglas S. Massey, "Manufacturing Marginality among Women and Latinos in Neo-liberal America," *Ethnic and Racial Studies* 17, no. 10 (2014): 1747–52; Douglas S. Massey, *Categorically Unequal: The American Stratification System* (New York: Russell Sage Foundation, 2007).

6. Pareene, "The Birthers: Who Are They and What Do They Want," *GAWKER*, July 22, 2009, http://gawker.com/5320465/the-birthers-who-are-they-and-what-do-they-want; Reeve Hamilton, "Berman's Agenda Leads Charge from the Right," *New York Times*, February 26, 2011.

7. Albert R. Hunt, "Republicans Ride Theories of the Fringe," *New York Times*, April 3, 2011.

8. Adam Liptak, "A Hint of New Life to a McCain Birth Issue," *New York Times*, July 11, 2008.

9. Eliza Collins, "Trump Questions Rubio's Eligibility," *Politico*, February 1, 2016.

10. "Transcript: Sixth Republican Top-Tier Debate 2016," *CBSNEWS*, January 15, 2016.

11. Sean Sullivan, Jenna Johnson, and Matea Gold, "The Rant That Could Derail Trump—and the GOP Rush to Get Him Back on Track," *Washington Post*, June 8, 2016.

12. Brent Kendall, "Trump Says Judge's Mexican Heritage Presents 'Absolute Conflict,'" *Wall Street Journal*, June 3, 2016.

26465411R00074

Made in the USA
Columbia, SC
10 September 2018